The Women's Millionaire Club

by Maureen G. Mulvaney, MGM

Join The Club!

www.TheWomensMillionaireClub.com

Copyright Page

Table of Contents

Dedication

The *Women's Millionaire Club* is dedicated to the loving, strong, confident and kind women who shaped and directed my life: my grandmother, Margaret McCormick Landry, and my mother, Mary Patricia Landry Mulvaney.

My grandmother and mother had a profound influence on my life. These remarkable women possessed the spirit to educate, empower and energize women to live their dreams. Everyone that knew them believed that their spirits would live on through my words, both spoken and written.

My grandmother was known as Madge. She was raised in Newfoundland, Canada, a providence often referred to as "a little slice of Ireland." Newfoundland is known for its fun-loving, high-spirited and deeply religious people. Grandmother was a lively, loving and devoutly Catholic woman who personified Newfoundland's reputation.

My grandmother always dreamed of living in America. Her cousins would say, *"Don't be so foolish, Madge, you come from a poor family that barely gets by. Your father is a fisherman, and there are many mouths to feed. Forget about America. Your job will be to care for your ma and pa when they can't work anymore. You'll just have to make a living here somehow."*

Her cousins' premonitions for the future proved correct, at least initially. Grandmother did work and care for her parents for most of her early adult life. Her only formal schooling was Tom's Dog, the third-grade reader she had completed in her one-room school in Newfoundland. Then, when she neared the age of 30, Grandmother was no longer able to find paying work in Newfoundland. Like so many others before her, she realized that she would have to go to America to help her family survive.

Although a life in America was her dream, leaving her family was painful. Grandmother knew she'd have to make her fortune in the new land so she'd be able to send money home to her beloved family and some day bring her loved ones to America one at a time.

With her goals for the future lodged firmly in her mind, Grandmother left her family in Newfoundland and boarded a train to Boston, Massachusetts. Being a proud young woman, she arrived in Boston wearing her finest clothes and a sealskin jacket. She made quite an impression as she stepped off the train wrapped in sealskins in the midst of a sweltering summer day. Curious onlookers pointed and smirked as the sweat dripped down her face, but Grandmother held her head high as she made her way to the boarding house, her first home in America.

Grandmother roomed with the other Canadians who had ventured to America in hopes of finding gold-lined streets and great fortune. Armed with her third-grade education,

Grandmother went to work as a domestic servant in the wealthy homes of Boston. Finding work was simple; wealthy families loved to hire Irish and Canadian immigrants, because they spoke English and worked hard.

Word spread throughout her boarding house that the domestic cooks made the best money. Although Grandmother could neither cook nor read the recipes very well, she aimed to be a cook so she could fulfill her dreams of bringing her family *"down to Boston."*

Her friends in the boarding house got her an interview with the head cook for a wealthy family. The head cook, who was also Canadian, needed an assistant cook. When the head cook inquired about her specialty, she replied, *"Well now, I come from Newfoundland and I can cook just about anything, but we cook a bit differently up there. If you'll just show me, one time, how the mistress likes her meals, I'll be doing it her way."* The head cook liked Grandmother's quick wit and easygoing sweet personality, and so she became the assistant to one of Boston's best cooks.

Soon after she arrived, the mistress of the house announced she'd be having an elaborate dinner party for the Boston elite. The whole kitchen was abuzz for weeks with preparations. On the day of the party, the highly stressed head cook instructed Grandmother to string the beans in the dining room. My grandmother had never heard this phrase before, but seeing that the head cook was too busy to explain, she did as she was told.

When the dinner began, the head cook was startled to hear the mistress scream, *"What is this?"* She ran to the dining room, where she found the Mrs. pointing in horror at the table. Grandmother had strung the green beans together in a necklace formation, and draped her creation around the table.

The head cook grabbed my grandmother by the arm and all but threw her through the dining room door. The mistress quickly followed. The head cook demanded to know what Grandmother had done with the beans. Fortunately, Grandmother was quick-witted and made up a story on the spot.

"Well now, up in Newfoundland, what we do is string the beans together like this to provide a ring of good luck for the entire family."

The mistress and the cook began to laugh, their anger quickly forgotten. The mistress returned to the dining room to regale her guest with the tale, and the guests toasted my grandmother for her gift of good luck. And with that, Grandmother became one of the beloved "characters of the house."

With her great sense of humor and vibrant personality, Madge made an impression wherever she went. Naturally, her friends tried to play matchmaker and fix Grandmother up with suitors. The logical choice was David – a dashing young single man from Nova Scotia who lived in the same boarding house as Grandmother. They were a match made in heaven, except that the young man was so homesick that he stayed in his room writing letters home to his mother all the time.

Grandmother's friends dared her to find a way to meet this charming young man: *"Madge, I bet you can't get him to come out of his room."* Grandmother took the dare.

There was a trellis over each door in the boarding house. One afternoon, the flap to the David's room was open. Grandmother stood on a chair and squirted water into his room. When he ran out shouting, *"Who ruined my letter to my mother?"* the assembled crowd began to laugh at point at Madge. David was soon smitten with this lively, sweet-natured beauty, and shortly thereafter, the two were married.

Curiously enough, David was also a cook. His kitchen was at sea, on a whaling ship. David spent half the year at sea and the other half at home. Because Madge had come from a family of seafaring men, she was used to managing the household until the men came home. My grandparents never found fame and fortune, but they made a warm and loving home together for more than 60 years.

Although David and Madge were never considered wealthy, my grandmother never forgot her dream of bringing her family from Canada to America. To raise money to bring relatives to the state, my grandmother frequently invited her

Canadian friends to "pass the hat" parties. These happy gatherings were filled with singing, dancing and plenty of laughter. Best of all, each party raised enough money to bring home another relative. My grandmother's dear parents soon joined her in Boston and lived with the couple until they passed on.

My mother was the second of eight children. She was named Mary Patricia, but everyone called her Marie. My mother was an active, vibrant baby until 19 months, when she was found crumpled in her crib like a rag doll. My poor Grandmother, who had seen the effects of infantile paralysis before, knew immediately that my mother had contracted the polio virus.

At the time, Dr. Jonas E. Salk had yet to invent the vaccine for polio, and there was no known cure. In 1919, the recommended treatment for the disease was the Iron Lung, followed by operations, braces and wheelchairs. My grandmother reluctantly placed my mother in the hospital, and visited every day to help care for her.

As the days grew into months, and the months into years, grandmother's family also grew. During the first 12 years of my mother's life, she was in and out of the hospital as the doctors experimented with the latest treatments. My grandmother's faith sustained her. She prayed for a miracle that would let her child walk again.

By the time my mother was 12, she had already undergone 26 operations on her bad leg. Despite these trials, my mother developed an incredibly sweet nature. My grandmother, who couldn't visit the hospital every day, would tell little Marie:

"Well, Marie...I love you, my dear, you're the sweetest thing in my life. You must understand that I can't come as much as I would like because I have to take care of your seven sisters and brothers. I want you to make your own fun by looking out the window, watch the birds and other animals run across the lawn. Wave to the people walking by. Enjoy every precious moment that God has given you. Even though money is tight, I've brought you a jar of olives. You can play 'Toss the Olives', with the other children, in the ward. Eat an olive and then toss the rest to the other children who don't have anyone to visit them.

I'll be back at the end of the week. In the meantime, ask God to grant you the Gift of Possibilities...TO MAKE THE IMPOSSIBLE POSSIBLE. Humbly ask God for the gift of motion so you can walk. I love you, my sweetheart. "

Little Marie took the words to heart. She gleefully waved and blew kisses at everyone that walked by the ward. The passersby would stop to talk to her and wish her well, and she never lacked for company.

One day, my mother's doctor stopped in to speak with her. Dr Legg sat on her bed to ask her if he could operate just one more time.

"Marie, I know we have tried 26 other times, but if you let me try one more time...a 27th operation, I believe I can fuse your ankle so you can walk. Would you let me try one more time?"

My mother took his face in her little hands and, with childlike wonderment, said,

"I'd let you try several more operations if you could just make me walk. I've prayed to God to guide your hands so you could give me the Gift of Possibilities...TO MAKE THE IMPOSSIBLE POSSIBLE. I trust you Dr. Legg. Sure, you can operate."

The doctor was so taken by this sweet child that he sobbed as he walked out of the room. His mission was to make her walk, and he succeeded. After the 27th surgery, my mother was finally able to walk without braces.

For the first time in her young life, my mother was finally able to go home for good. Her homecoming, however, was bitter sweet. Mother had always been sheltered and protected in the hospital and never realized that she was different from others. On her first day home, she wanted nothing more to show her aunt and cousins how well she could walk without the use of crutches or braces. My mother begged and pleaded with her mother to let her make the short walk down to her aunt's house.

Grandmother was hesitant to grant my mother's request, because she knew how cruel kids could be – but my mother's excitement overshadowed these concerns, and Grandmother finally relented. Grandmother's concerns, however, were justified. As Mother made the trip to her aunt's home, the neighbor kids came out to taunt her. They started calling her *"limpy, gimpy cripple"* and mocking her awkward steps.

Little Marie had never heard such hurtful phrases before, and she became frightened by the torments. She tried to run away, but her legs collapsed beneath her, and she fell to the ground. The cruel children picked up rocks and started stoning my mother until her aunt came out and picked her up off the ground.

The saying, *"Sticks and stones may break my bones but names will never hurt me,"* couldn't be more wrong. The physical pain the children had inflicted on my mother dissipated quickly – but the names stuck. My mother felt like a second-class citizen, until my grandmother stepped in to explain how brave and courageous her young daughter had been.

Grandmother explained that the other children would never have been able to handle the pain and suffering my mother had endured with such a positive spirit. Through my grandmother's kind words, my mother was empowered, and her self-confidence returned.

My mother was her vibrant, happy self when she met my father at the age of 18. Father was a sailor from Michigan who was stationed in Boston. Mother and Father had a whirlwind romance. World War II was on the verge of erupting, and my father wanted to marry my mother before the war broke out. He spent two long days trying to convince my grandmother to give him permission to wed my mother. His persistence paid off; my grandmother realized the futility of her protests, and the two were quickly married.

My parents were deeply in love – best friends who admired and respected each other. For seven years, they grew as a couple and prayed for the gift of children. Their wishes were granted with the birth of my brother Paul Wayne, my sister Susan, and me. During my birth, the doctors accidentally nicked my mother's kidney, causing her to become very ill. Mom named me Maureen Gail Mulvaney, because Maureen is a lyrical, Irish name – and because my initials would be MGM ... her Big Production.

My father was often away at sea, but mother took care of her family with confidence and courage. She raised us with sheer joy, love and tenderness. Mother taught us space repetition from the beginning: *if you see something, hear something, or say something six times a day for 21 days, you own it, whether you like it or not.*

My mother's practice of space repetition was effective. When she noticed my brother's proclivity and talent with his hands, she took to saying, *"Oh Wayne, you're so good with your hands,"* as often as possible. Wayne grew up to be a plumber for the US Air Force.

Mother would tell my sister, *"Oh Susan, you are so good with numbers."* Susan grew up to work in Congressional records for the Environmental Protection Agency and worked with the US Congress.

Mother would tell me, *"Oh MGM, I always knew you would be a big production one day."* With encouragement like that, is it any wonder that I grew up to be an international speaker and author? My siblings' successes and my success were direct results of the positive spaced repetition education that my mother gave us.

To this day, I will not set foot on a stage to begin a speaking engagement without basking in my mother's energy as she spoke these words:

> *"Dear Lord, please give your blessing to my dear daughter on this day. May the strength of God guide you and give you his words of wisdom so that you will remain calm and be able to deliver your speech without any flaws. Just remember that I am there with you on stage and that my LOVE is like a warm and sheltering cloak around you. Your Loving Mother."*

It is with love and gratitude that I dedicate this book to my grandmother and my mother. These remarkable women gave all of their energy to providing their families with the *education* needed to be successful. They *empowered* us with their words and deeds and *energized* with their incredible spirits.

As long as I am alive, the spirits of my mother and grandmother will survive. With their strength behind me, I have dedicated myself to ensuring that women's natural traits and abilities are honored, nurtured, and seen as powerful tools to bring our dreams to life with the Gift of Possibilities … to make the impossible possible.

This book honors and celebrates those women with the same spirit that my beloved mother and grandmother possessed. This book is for all of the women who demonstrate the courage, strength, kindness and humility that make us who we are.

My vision for *The Women's Millionaire Club* is to "educate, empower and energize all home-based businesswomen."

My mission: to create more conscientious women millionaires who will make a difference on Planet Earth in a kind, loving and fun manner.

The Women's Millionaire Club is a dream come true. *The Gift of Possibility* was opened for me – now I'd like to pass that Gift on to you. I can still feel my grandmother and mother's sweet spirits whispering, *"I believe in YOU. This is your destiny. Claim your destiny."*

I hope you will be educated, empowered and energized by the tools and stories you find in this book. Most of all, I hope you feel the spirit of this book. The time has come to celebrate and honor women. I believe in you! Claim your destiny!

The Secret Recipe For SUCCESS!

·KNOW WHAT YOU WANT.
Explore and clarify your thoughts.

·BELIEVE YOU CAN HAVE IT.
Examine and understand your beliefs and feelings.

·TAKE ACTION.
Learn to act appropriately and consistently.

·GIVE THANKS.
Appreciate your results.

Part I –

The World of Women Millionaires

Introduction

You are reading this book because you have an unquenchable thirst to live the American dream – a lifestyle of financial and literal freedom that creates abundance in all areas of your life. You have a desire to live the lifestyle of the rich and famous, to have the cars, the clothes, the houses, the money, the vacations and the time to enjoy life.

Like you, I've always been fascinated with finding a way to attract success, wealth, abundance and prosperity into my life. For years, my life has been a personal quest to uncover the secrets and the tricks, the easy ways to acquire wealth and to find the time to enjoy its trappings.

The following statement set me on fire: *Women comprise 56% of Americans over the age of 18 who live in poverty.*

The mere thought of so many women living in poverty shocked me and fueled my passion to share and help others. I wanted to help others, create abundance and demonstrate the possibilities of financial and time freedom. The solution was clear: I needed to write a book that explored the traits and recipes of successful women, so readers could emulate and achieve similar results.

Travel with me Back in Time

Let's play the "Who Am I?" game. Read the following paragraph, then use your imagination to picture and describe the person to which it alludes.

> *I am a top executive in a very large organization. Thousands of people join my team and follow my lead. I travel the world for business and pleasure and speak to groups both large and small. I live a dream lifestyle. I am a millionaire. Who Am I?*

When I posed this description to my friends, family and strangers off the street, every one of them described the same person: a male baby boomer. Is that the person you instantly imagined?

Most of us automatically think of men when we think of millionaires. This disposition comes from a lifetime of seeing men take the top positions in industry and government and make the big bucks.

All my career role models were men. My first boss was a man. When I asked him what traits would help me get to the top, he didn't hesitate to explain that I'd have to be more like a man to get ahead in the business world. He told me that dominance and control were the main traits that were honored in the workplace.

The patterns of success were spelled out in all the hunting and sports terms he spouted daily: *Stalk your prey, destroy them before they destroy you, dominate the situation, go in for the kill and bring home a trophy.*

This terminology seemed foreign to me, but all the men in the office knew how to negotiate with this hunter/sportsman phraseology. Most of the men had grown up playing "shoot-'em up" with little cowboy men or green army soldiers and all had played on sports team at one time or another.

The games of my childhood were very different from those of my male counterparts. I didn't play with little green army men or play team sports, which centered on taking control and dominating the field. My childhood was filled with games of jump rope, hop*scotch*, and baby doll games. My girlfriends would hold the rope, while I jumped to my own tune and with my own set of rules. The traits I learned from these games centered on collaboration and connection, not control and dominance.

The 1970's Women's Liberation changed everything. We were told that we could do anything and be anything. We were taught the mantra, *"I am woman, hear me roar."* We flocked to the business world, knowing that we could have anything we desired. This was a new day with a new way of doing business. We were told that we had *"come a long way, baby."* Perhaps women would begin to be honored for their unique traits and talents in the workplace.

Fast Forward to the 21 Century

To begin writing this book, I researched other books that were in the bookstores. I started with a book entitled *The Millionaire Next Door,* by Thomas J. Stanley, PhD and William D Danko, PhD. To my astonishment, no woman was mentioned in the entire book. From the perspectives of the male authors, the only millionaires who *"lived next door"* were men. Since I could not relate to any of the people in the book, I soon lost interest. I decided to write my own book from a female perspective.

I wanted to write a book to honor the traits that women bring to the table – collaboration, connection and support. I wanted to write a book that included the Recipes of Success to show others that, with practice, anyone can model the actions of these women and can achieve the same results.

I looked at my corporate female friends in hopes of finding role models for other women. Unfortunately, my corporate friends were not the kind of role models that I had envisioned. They had specific college education backgrounds, worked at least 80 hours per week, and felt frustrated by lack of family time. These women were disgruntled by having to work twice as hard in order to be considered half as capable as their male counterparts. They also complained about being considered weak if they managed their 'shops' the way they wanted to.

These women were bruised and bloody from hitting their heads on the glass ceiling. My belief that women had shattered the glass ceiling in the 1970s was crushed.

I turned to successful female small business owners. Perhaps they could be role models for other women. Unfortunately, these women worked 24 hours a day and seven days a week. They dealt with employees who either did not come to work or quit without notice. A huge amount of capital was needed for start-up fees and ongoing fees. Furthermore, they had no family time or vacation time. Many complained about having to dominate the marketplace and fight fierce competition in order to survive. These business strategies were the same "control and dominate" approaches that my previous employer had touted.

I felt certain that some industry existed in which women could use their traits to create wealth, live a free lifestyle, and still have time for faith, family and fun. Then, my successful female entrepreneur friends exposed me to the world of Direct Selling. They owned home-based businesses that did not require specific educational backgrounds. A massive amount of start-up money was not needed. These women managed their own time. They took trips to the Bahamas and other exotic places, all with their families in tow.

When asked about her job, my entrepreneurial friend smiled and said, *"I meet new people and make connections. I share my products and ideas. I show others how to be financially free. I spend a portion of every day in personal development, so I can be the best leader I can be. I love what I do."*

These strong and confident women opened the door to a whole new world of opportunities for me. Direct sales proved to be an industry in which women could learn and embrace the Secrets of Financial and Time Freedom and could create abundance BY BEING THEMSELVES.

In 2000, corporate women still only earned 75 cents to every dollar that a man earned. Yet, home-based businesses are free from that glass ceiling. These women simply laugh and say, *"The sky is the limit for us. If friends and family members want to go to the top, they can just roll up their sleeves and dive in. We can all get there together."*

This team unity approach was completely the opposite of the "controlling and dominating" ideals of men. These entrepreneurial women, on the other hand, created teams of volunteers that work together.

One woman asked, *"How long would volunteers stay around if we demanded and commanded? My job is to lead, motivate, inspire and empower others. By nurturing and showing others how to grow, we can all succeed."* This support spirit is what women bring to the business world.

The Women's Millionaire Club, is about the remarkable women who rule in an industry where there is no glass ceiling. The playing field is even, so women make the same amount as men. If gender is not a factor, why are these women so successful? Are they genetically superior? Do they come from influential families? Do they have exceptional education backgrounds? Do their ages matter? Is the food they eat important?

This book began as my own personal journey to find truth. I can now share the Gift of Possibilities with other women. Through this book, readers will discover how these women achieved their success. Anytime you have a clear goal in mind, the universe seemingly provides the means of reaching that goal. My goal was to determine how average women could become millionaires. Twenty-one female millionaires gave me the opportunity to conduct surveys, assessments and interviews with them in order to uncover the secrets of how they attained success. The women agreed, because they are interested in helping others reach the top.

The heartwarming and touching profiles of each woman show how they overcame numerous challenges. Some were fortunate enough to find mentors immediately. Others relied on books and tapes. Most wished for a female mentor. Now, these women can be mentors for any reader with high hopes for success.

I hope that this honest and practical guide can enable these women to be mentors for other women. My greatest desire is that through reading these stories and strategies for success, women can pave a smooth and short road to the top.

1 – The Recipe for Success

The American Dream is a hope for people around the world. Many great-grandparents and grandparents blazed the trail to the shores of America to give the Gift of Possibilities to their children. The Gift of Possibilities, or the ability to make the impossible possible, has an exact Success Recipe.

Follow the Recipe

Have you ever prepared a dish that did not turn out well? Perhaps an ingredient was left out or improperly substituted for another ingredient. Perhaps you followed the steps of the recipe in the incorrect order. Like any recipe, the Recipe for Success has a specific order and number of ingredients that must be used. The recipe can only be enhanced when the basics are included.

People generally want immediate results. They want "get rich quick" short cuts. Television shows document the everyday lives of famous celebrities, purchasing Louis Vuitton handbags and Jimmy Choo shoes. Viewers stay glued to the screen, searching for tips on how to become rich as well. They want the end results as fast as possible.

The 'Get-Rich-Quick' Fantasy

Most people want to "get rich quick" and fantasize about winning the lottery. In fact, in many states, the lottery is called Fantasy. This is not a coincidence.

Evelyn Adams won the New Jersey lottery not once, but twice. In 1985 and 1986, she won a total of $5.4 million. Winning the lottery twice is a dream for most people. Evelyn's life, however, is not as wonderful as expected. She is penny-less and lives in a trailer. Now in the victim role, Evelyn shares her sad story with anyone willing to listen. She says, "Everybody wanted my money. Everybody had their hands out." Evelyn gambled with her winnings and lost everything.

Another 'get rich quick' enthusiast is Janite Lee. In 1993, Janite wanted to use her $18 million prize to help others. She shared her wealth with various charitable organizations, and in less than a decade, she filed for bankruptcy as well.

Lottery Mentality

Evelyn, Janite and countless others believed in the short cut to wealth. They spent their winnings and did not stay rich for long.

'Doing' is only one part of the Recipe for Success. Evelyn and Janite became momentary millionaires, because they did not know the entire Recipe for Success. They used only a part of the Success Recipe. Their momentary success was constricting instead of freeing and did not last long.

The facts published by the Lottery itself are quite clear: single state lotteries usually have odds of approximately 18 million to one, while multiple state lotteries have odds as high as 120 million to one. A 1999 study conducted by the Consumer Federation of America and the financial services firm Primerica found the following results:

Forty percent of Americans with incomes between $25,000 and $35,000 and nearly one-half of respondents with an income of $15,000 to $25,000 believe winning the lottery would provide enough for retirement. **A third of Americans believe that winning the lottery is the only way to become financially secure in life.**

Twenty percent of lottery players contribute to 82% of lottery's revenue. These players are disproportionately low-income, minority men who have less than a college education.

Overall, 27% of respondents said that their best chance to gain $500,000 in their lifetime was through a sweepstakes or lottery win.

The Lottery Recipe
Mix   Fantasy Thinking
Add   'Lady Luck' Beliefs
Add   Consumer Buy, Buy, Buy Actions
Cooks up a: Batch of Disaster

Fantasy Thinking
People deny facts and revert to childhood fantasies. In many ways, the lottery is the adult version of Santa Claus – both are unrealistic dreams with no basis in reality.

Winning the lottery appears to be the ultimate short cut to financial success, magically making life easier. "Get rich quick" enthusiasts think, "I'll win the lottery and make millions."

'Lady Luck' Beliefs

Seeing others win huge lottery prizes creates a flood of positive emotions, cementing the irrational belief that some people are just lucky. However, luck is not a personal attribute that only some have. The "get rich quick" enthusiast believes in luck as a key element of success.

'Big Bucks Consumer' Actions

To fulfill the "get rich quick" fantasy, people take action. They continue to spend, buy and consume nonstop. This book cannot help those who want to "get rich quick" with a lottery mentality. If you are willing to learn a new way of thinking and to embrace a reliable Recipe for Success, this book can be of use.

Back to Science 101:

A one-time occurrence is called an INCIDENT.
A two-time occurrence is called a COINCIDENCE.
A three-time occurrence is called a LAW.

In order for the average person to use the Law of Success, the results must be replicated successfully.

The Women's Millionaire Club is a book about the Law of Success that the top performers follow. They are the Women Millionaires of the home-based business industry. If one woman were to become a millionaire, that would be an INCIDENT. If two women were to become millionaires, that would be a COINCIDENCE. However, if three or more women become millionaires, that is a LAW.

The Women's Millionaire Club currently has over 20 members who have become millionaires through their home-based businesses. When these women became millionaires, they demonstrated the Success Law IN ACTION.

Knowing the traits of women who are already successful and their Recipes of Success can guide you down the same path. However, this path does require appropriate, consistent action. Whatever your situation, this book can show you the secret ingredients and traits of the millionaires who follow a consistent Recipe for Success.

A Success Bite

Follow the Women's
Millionaire Club
Recipes for Success.
Make the Impossible,
Possible.

---

2 – The History of Network Marketing

A common myth is that home-based businesses are pyramid schemes. How did this myth arise? History can reveal the answer.

New Ideas and Concepts Create Resistance

Humans tend to resist change. New ideas, concepts or methods are often ridiculed. Breakthroughs in medicine, science, art or business go through a process of opposition. First, when a person is presented with an unusual or revolutionary new idea, they tend to laugh or ridicule the idea. Then, they watch intently to see if the idea will work. As it begins to work by improving their life, the idea gains acceptance and often replaces the original concept.

A Medical Breakthrough

In 1919, my mother contracted infantile paralysis, more commonly known as polio. Before Jonas E. Sulk developed a vaccine to wipe out polio, the disease devastated many families. Physicians had no ideas on how to attack the disease. They treated polio by isolating the affected limb and placing it in a brace, which usually atrophied the muscles and reduced or eliminated mobility. Although it was ineffective, this was the accepted medical treatment at the time.

An Australian nurse, Elizabeth Kenny, developed a treatment method that involved massage and manipulation. Her method helped patients recover from the disease with full mobility and no residual effects. Instead of being heralded for her revolutionary idea, she was met with ridicule, stubborn resistance and outright opposition. She was quickly labeled a heretic.

More than thirty years after her initial findings were chronicled in several books, Elizabeth Kenny's story was portrayed through film. Entitled *And They Shall Walk Again*, the film alerted the public to her miraculous treatment. Once viewers saw children who were once paralyzed learn to walk without crutches, they were astonished. Parents demanded that physicians use Kenny's treatment methods on their children.

Sister Kenny, as she was called, had a revolutionary idea that created great resistance and opposition. Once Elizabeth Kenny's non-traditional treatment demonstrated successful results, the treatment spread rapidly.

A Business Breakthrough

In 1858, a Nantucket Quaker named Rowland Hussey Macy wanted out of the whaling industry. He pursued a career in business and opened several unsuccessful small shops. He then had the revolutionary idea of opening a 'fancy dry goods' store on 6th Avenue in New York City. The store eventually became the successful department store Macy's. An adventurous young lad on the whaling ship, Emily Morgan, had had a red star tattooed on his hand. As a tribute to his past, Macy chose a red star as the symbol for his new store.

Macy's grew so quickly that Rowland bought the adjoining buildings and kept adding departments. Macy's quickly became one of the largest stores in the world. This new 'department style' of running a business started to spread around the nation.

As with Kenny's case, Rowland's revolutionary idea faced serious opposition. Small, family-owned shops were being threatened. The shop owners vehemently opposed the growth of the department stores.
In a desperate attempt to rally the public, shop owners from New York and Chicago banded together in protest. However, these protests were short lived, as consumers realized that department stores were better ways to do business. For the first time, buyers had a convenient way to purchase various different items under one roof.

A Direct Selling Breakthrough
Direct selling dates back centuries. The pilgrims brought it to the shores of America. Individual sales clerks, known as "Yankee Peddlers," went from door to door selling tools and wares. When families began to move west, the peddlers packed up their wares in wagons and traveled around the countryside to sell directly to groups of families.

By the late 1800's, resistance grew as department stores, family-owned retail shops, and mail order houses directly competed with the peddlers. Some peddlers saw an opportunity to compete as a sales force.

At the beginning of the 20th century, Henry Heinz, a former peddler, started his own company. He made vegetable products, such as ketchup and pickles, to sell to consumers who were unable to grow vegetables on their own. He formed an organized sales force of 400 sales clerks.

In 1886, another former peddler named Asa Candler bought the formula for Coca Cola from pharmacist John Pemberton. He also created a sales force to sell the Coke syrup to restaurants.

David H. McConnell created a massive sales force for his California Perfume Company – 10,000 sales representatives who sold over 117 different products. In 1939, the California Perfume Company transformed into Avon Products, Inc.

Another well-known peddler, Alfred C. Fuller, conceived the idea of salespeople owning their own businesses, as dealers, with a revolutionary new business plan: commission sales. He founded the Fuller Brush Company and sold cleaning products through home demonstrations. Fuller hired 270 dealers that earned commission on their sales. The Fuller Brush Company thrived and brought in an unprecedented $1 million in 1919. Fuller's company became the model for almost all future direct sales companies.

America was expanding – and so was the direct sales industry. Direct sales were rapidly evolving - from individual peddlers to sales forces to owner dealers.

By the 1920's, resistance from retail stores intensified. Door-to-door salespeople sold everything from cooking utensils to cosmetics. Retail stores fought back and enlisted the help of local governments. New laws were passed to prevent door-to-door sales. The Federal Government imposed new regulations that clarified the relationship between companies and employees. Sales clerks became independent contractors and bought the products for resale. This new standard calmed the resistance for a time.

In 1931, a former Fuller Brush Sales Vice President named Frank Stanley Beveridge joined forces with Catherine L. O'Brien to form the Stanley Home Products Company. Their vision was based on the Fuller Brush Company model and shaped by the hardships of the Great Depression.

With 25% of the nation out of work, Catherine and Frank wanted people to have the opportunity to start their own low-investment business selling practical products that every household needed, such as mops, brushes and cleaners. As the Depression raged on, some innovative salespeople gave demonstrations at club and organization meetings to increase sales. Sales boomed as a result.

Other salespeople improved upon the idea even further and began inviting friends and family members over for home demonstrations. Tough times created a perfect solution to boost income and the 'party plan' was born.

In 1934, Carl F. Rehnborg, founder of the California Vitamins Corporation, noticed two patterns in his sales force. First, most new sales representatives were friends of existing salespeople who wanted the products at wholesale cost. This form of sales became affectionately known as 'friendship marketing.' Second, Carl discovered that creating a sales force of many people who each sold a small amount was more profitable than depending on a few high-selling superstars.

Carl combined these two ideas and designed a new sales compensation plan to encourage salespeople to enlist friends and family members as sales representatives. California Vitamins rewarded representatives for their personal sales as well as those produced by their network of sales representatives. The sales force expanded exponentially, creating a quick and efficient distribution channel that eliminated the middleman.

California Vitamins was renamed the NutraLite™ Food Supplement Corporation. The company contracted with Mytinger & Casselberry to become the exclusive American distributor of NutraLite™ products. As a result, the first documented compensation plan for sales and distribution emerged. Today, this sales strategy is known as Multi-Level Marketing (MLM), or Network Marketing.

In the MLM/Network Marketing industry, individuals with no prior business experience could become "distributors." Distributors could buy products at a 35% discount and sell for a retail profit. To encourage sales, NutraLite™ paid distributors a monthly bonus of 25% of the total sales. A distributor who enlisted 25 customers was promoted to Direct Distributor. This gave the distributor the opportunity to enlist other sellers. Those Direct Distributors who amassed 150 customers were paid a bonus of 2% on the total sales volume. Dr. Forrest Shaklee saw a new form of personal distribution for his food supplements and joined NutraLite™ in 1956.

Loosely based on the Fuller Brush Company's 'own-your-own business' strategy, this new sales compensation plan motivated distributors to enlist and train other sellers. The Great Depression spurred the innovation and success of network marketing. As joblessness rose, so did network marketing. The industry provided hope during desperate times. Many

> # A Success Bite
>
> "New Ideas are met with Resistance, which becomes Acceptance, with your Persistence."
> ~MGM
> 1. People will Laugh
> 2. People will Watch
> 3. People will Follow You To Success!

flocked to their only opportunity to own a business, work from home, and earn an income based on personal responsibility.

The following well-known companies were highly influenced by this era of scarcity. Their leaders were expansive thinkers and innovators looking to provide an equal opportunity for the average person to control their destiny by owning a home-based business.

- In 1945, Brownie Wise and Earl Tupper founded Tupperware™.
- In 1956, Jan and Frank Day founded Jafra Cosmetics™.
- In 1957, Mary Crowley founded Home Interiors™.
- In 1963, Mary Kay Ash founded Mary Kay Cosmetics™.
- After World War II, two high school friends returned from the war and joined the NutraLite™ team. By 1959, they founded their own company called Amway™, the American way of marketing products. Amway grew quickly and took over NutraLite™ in 1972.

Near the end of World War I, network-marketing companies boomed by helping many create badly needed additional income. Huge exponential growth was the natural outcome. Unscrupulous characters also saw an opportunity to abuse this new business structure to create the "get rich quick" schemes that would plaque the industry for years.

45

The chain letter was one of the first abuses of exponential growth that criminals used to generate income.

Chain letters started in Denver, Colorado, in 1935 and spread rapidly. Their

messages encouraged the recipient to pass copies of the letter on to as many people as possible. Manipulative fabrications were included in the letters, threatening the recipient with bad luck, physical violence or death for breaking the chain.

Chain letters were the ultimate "get rich quick" pyramid schemes. They played off the success of network marketing, but the colossal difference was these pyramid schemes did not offer a product or a service and were doomed to implode and fail.

Criminals quickly found a way to profit from the chain letter. First, they renamed chain letters the 'Prosperity Club' or 'Send-a-Dime' letters. Second, they requested money or other valuable items to participate. Third, they offered a substantial return to recruit other people, an idea borrowed from network marketing. For every new recruit, participant earned a small amount and moved up a level in the company.

Participants at the top of the pyramid earned money from thousands of people below.

The Denver post office was flooded with thousands of letters before the chain spread to other cities. The US post office estimated that over 10 million chain letters were mailed each day during the 1930s. Some letters were harmful and fraudulent. Postal authorities joined forces with law enforcement agencies to crack down on the chain letter phenomenon. The crackdown, combined with more prosperous times, lessened the popularity of chain letters in the 1940s.

Nevertheless, pyramid schemes were so lucrative they morphed into larger schemes. Criminals used pyramids to form companies that blurred the line between the legitimate direct selling method and illegitimate pyramid schemes.

Legitimate Network Marketing versus Pyramid Schemes

Legitimate network marketing companies allow entrepreneurs to grow a home-based business by selling products or services

A Success Bite

A Pyramid Scheme requires constant recruitment, offers no products or services, has a minimal chance of payment .

People rarely receive a payment before the pyramid implodes.

directly to others and recruiting customers to do the same. These individuals earn an income through the sale of valid, viable products or services.

Pyramid schemes, on the other hand, offer no products or services. These schemes require people to recruit, recruit, recruit – or purchase enormous amounts of worthless products.

Although the two are distinctly different businesses, individuals and law enforcement agencies struggled to differentiate legitimate companies from fraudulent ones. In 1974, Senator Walter Mondale declared that these fraudulent pyramid companies were the nation's number one form of consumer fraud. The Federal Trade Commission (FTC) and other law enforcement agencies quickly stepped in to clean up the abuses. However, these agencies began their "clean-up" operations without a clear picture of what constituted abuse.

In order to demonstrate their commitment to eradicate pyramid schemes, the FTC and other law enforcement agencies began indiscriminately targeting almost all network-marketing companies. The allegations reached a fever pitch when the FTC filed formal charges against the largest target: the Amway Company.

The FTC deemed Amway an illegal pyramid because the company's products were not sold in retail stores, which they said constituted a restraint of trade, and because the organization's distributors earned money by recruiting new distributors.

Amway™ (and NutriLite™) was desperate to clear the company's name. They spent four long years and millions of dollars in legal fees to prove they were not a pyramid scheme, but

---

A Success Bite

The FTC acknowledged that Network Marketing is a **LEGAL** and **EFFICIENT Distribution System** of legitimate products and or services.

---

in fact a legitimate company. Amway ultimately won the lawsuit, and the FTC acknowledged in its ruling that **network marketing was a legal and efficient distribution system.**

3 - Home-Based Businesses Today

To avoid confusion, I will use the term home-based business to include MLM, network marketing and direct selling. Today, home-based businesses bring together independent business people with common interests. The entrepreneurial spirit the members embody has empowered them, and the belief that people can create their own destiny is apparent in these organizations.

Distributors, consultants and representatives are given the opportunity to start a small business, which they can choose to grow into a large business, by sharing their experience and quality products with others. Home-based businesses offer great opportunities to all people, without discrimination, and emphasize that the individual makes the difference in achieving success.

The home-based business industry has again gained favor as a way to cushion the financial blows of an erratic world economy. In fact, Warren Buffet, Paul Zane Pilzer, Robert Kiyosaki, and Donald Trump all advocate home-based businesses as a way to achieve wealth.

Paul Zane Pilzer, author of *The Next Millionaires* and *The Wellness Revolution,* said, "Of all the entrepreneurial opportunities available today, one of the most important is direct selling, also called network marketing. The industry is perfectly poised to create many of the next millionaires.

Billionaire investor Warren Buffet has said the network marketing company he purchased was the best investment decision he'd ever made.

Robert Kiyosaki, author of *Rich Dad, Poor Dad,* says, "The richest people in the world build networks, everyone else looks for work. A network marketing business is a new and revolutionary way to achieve wealth."

Kim Kiyosaki, author of *Rich Woman*, says, "I believe the world would be a better place if there were more Rich Women. There is a Rich Woman inside EVERY woman."

Diane Kennedy, author of *Loopholes of the Rich,* says, "One of the biggest benefits of having a business is getting a bunch of write-offs that you just can't get as an employee. You could join a MLM, and do it the right way, to immediately establish a legitimate business."

In *Why We Want You To Be Rich,* Donald Trump says, "Network marketing has proven itself to be a viable and rewarding source of income. There have been remarkable examples of success."

Fortune magazine has called direct selling, "The best kept secret in the business world. It has experienced a 94% growth in the last 10 years, with annual sales in excess of $30 billion in the US and $100 billion worldwide. Financial experts say it's a 'recession-proof industry.'"

The home-based business industry is thriving, as evidenced by the women millionaires featured in this book. A home-based business is an excellent way to become wealthy, especially for those willing to put in the effort.

The home-based business industry places responsibility squarely on the shoulders of each individual. As such, anyone interested in joining a home-based business must diligently research the prospective organization she wishes to join. One of the best places to start learning about the industry is the Direct Selling Association.

The Direct Selling Association

The Direct Selling Association (DSA) was formed in Binghamton, New York, in 1910 to look after the needs of the 93,000 traveling salesmen and their companies. The purpose of the DSA was to protect, promote and police the direct-selling industry by making sure ethical business methods were observed.

DSA began with 10 member companies. The organization has since expanded to include more than 211 member companies. Companies may only be admitted to the association after a yearlong period during which "the company's business plan is reviewed to verify compliance with all provisions of DSA's Code of Ethics. At present, only companies with direct selling operation in the U.S. are eligible for membership."

What is a Home-Based Business?

Direct selling companies sell products or services directly to individuals. For a minimal investment, each person may join a direct selling company as an independent representative, distributor or consultant and become a home-based business owner.

As an independent contractor, the individual owns a business and gains the associated tax benefits; however, the main company offers education, office support and technical product support. The individual sells or shares products and services with their network of family, friends and colleagues, and encourages others to join them in the advantages of

---

A Success Bite

Advantages of a home-based business:

- Minimal Investment
- Tax Benefits
- Company Support
- Business Ownership

---

home-business ownership. As people join, the organization grows and everyone benefits from additional income, quality products and social connections. The original 'friendship marketing' drives the organization.

How Many People Are In the Home-Based

Business Industry?

According to the DSA, an estimated 15 million people are involved in direct selling in the U.S., with more than 68 million participants worldwide. Approximately 90 percent of all direct selling independent contractors operate their businesses part-time.

A Success Bite

The vast majority of home-based business owners are women (87.9%). Men or two-person teams such as couples comprise a third of the industry (12.1%)

-2007 DSA Study

The industry is growing and sales are increasing. Approximately 74% of the American public has purchased goods or service through direct selling. Worldwide sales are now over $112 billion.

What and Why do People Buy through Direct Sales?
People purchase everything from soup to nuts through direct selling. The most common reasons people give for buying directly from a home-based business are:

- Superior product quality
- Money-back guarantees
- A salesperson who demonstrates and explains the product's uses and benefits

Common Reasons for Joining Home-Based Businesses

Because the industry offers many different incentives, people join the industry for many different reasons. Members of home-based businesses join for one of seven specific reasons:

Wholesale Discounts: People who join a company to purchase products at wholesale cost and enjoy a discount.

Specific Objectives: People who join a company to purchase gifts at a discount or earn a small income to meet a specific need. These people often quit after that goal is met.

Quality of Life Improvement: People who join a company to earn extra income. They do not wish to give up their day job, they just want extra income.

Social Contacts: People who join a company to connect with others and have a richer social life.

Recognition: People who join a home-based business to gain recognition and appreciation.

Benefits: People who join a company to gain the significant tax and financial benefits of owning a home-based business.

Career: People who join a company to own a home-based business. Only 7.5% of people in the home-based business industry work 40 or more hours per week, yet these people earn significant incomes.

The majority of home-based business owners work part time to earn a supplemental income source. Let's look at some industry statistics:

- 25% of full-time sales people (approximately 8% of the field) grossed $100,000 or more annually
- 50% work less than 10 hours per week
- 40% work less than 5 hours per week

Why are Home-Based Businesses a Good Opportunity for Women?

Women comprise more than 85% of the home-based business industry. Home-based businesswomen do not need specific educational or experience requirements to join the direct sales industry. Start-up costs are minimal, generally less than $150. The tax benefits, especially during the first three years, usually offset the initial start-up costs.

Furthermore, home-based businesses offer:

- Unlimited possibilities – no glass ceiling
- An even playing field – women earn the same income as men, dollar for dollar
- No discrimination – no matter your age, ethnic background or disability, there is room for you in a home-based business.

- 8% of the industry is over age 65
- 7% of the industry has a physical disability
- 13% of the industry is African American
- 13% of the industry is Hispanic American
- 6% of the industry is Asian American

The Age of the Entrepreneur

Paul Zane Pilzer predicts that we are now entering the Age of the Entrepreneur. His research shows:

> *Not only have changing tax laws leveled the playing field, but also changes in technology have actually tilted that field toward individual entrepreneurs, giving them the distinct edge. Home-Based Businesses are one of the fastest growing segments in our economy, and that trend will only continue, as the age of the corporation, which began barely a century ago, now gives way to the age of the entrepreneur.*

> *Among many other forms of entrepreneurial enterprise, the modern direct selling industry is perfectly poised to flourish in the environment and offer unprecedented opportunity to an unprecedented number of people.*

> *The Age of the Entrepreneur: Enormous personal wealth but also the affirmation and strengthening of moral and family values, as well as personal and societal freedoms, that come with owning your own*

business and controlling your own destiny. In direct selling companies, you can 'have your cake and eat it too' by entering an already established and proven field or industry while still owning your own business.

Democratization of Wealth

Pilzer explains that the democratization of wealth is happening because huge corporations are giving way to the individual entrepreneurs. The Small Business Association reported that small businesses account for more than one-half of the nation's economic output and employ more than one-half of our private-sector workforce. To break down the numbers even further, Home-Based Businesses account for fully one-half of all small businesses in operation today.

"In the past, where we'd see a single company going to $1billion, today we'll more likely see 1,000 individuals each going to $1 million. Instead, of the rich getting richer, it means there are more people getting rich: the number of millionaires is increasing," Pilzer said.

Overcoming the Misconceptions

In the beginning of this project, I didn't know what I'd discover regarding the home-based business industry. Like so many of you, my concepts of the industry were not entirely positive. Although I didn't know exactly what a pyramid scheme was, network marketing seemed to fit the bill.

I now see that the home-based business industry gets a bum rap. Yes, there were abuses in the industry, but those abuses exist in every industry (Enron immediately springs to mind). I learned that the home-based business industry is not a pyramid scheme. In my opinion, the real pyramids are the school systems, government agencies and large corporations.

When I was a teacher, my school system only had one superintendent. No matter how much education, experience or talent I possessed, getting to the top of the pyramid was not possible. The position was locked up until the superintendent died or decided to retire. The school system was a pyramid, with the superintendent at the top and us worker-bee teachers at the bottom.

In a home-based business, on the other hand, you can get to the top and bring others along with you. You don't just have one person at the top, you have as many as are willing to do the work to get there.

The women of this book prove my point. They range from 29 to 69. Can you imagine a 70 year old being able to become a Millionaire with Wal-Mart? At Wal-Mart, she is invited to be a greeter. In the home-based business arena, she is extended the opportunity to become a Millionaire.

Home-based businesses are the perfect industry for women. With no glass ceiling, dollar for dollar compensation, no age limits, no physical disability limits and no ethnic limits, the possibilities are truly LIMITLESS.

A Success Bite

The home-based business industry is a
Gift of Possibilities ...
the Impossible,
Becomes Possible.

4 – The Women's Millionaire Club Survey

The women millionaires surveyed in this chapter were randomly chosen from six different companies within the direct selling industry. Twenty-one of those women became members of the Women's Millionaire club and are featured in this book.

My primary criteria for the Women's Millionaire Club membership were simple. Each candidate had to have become a millionaire from the income she earned in her home-based direct sales business.

My background in psychology, coupled with intense curiosity, made me wonder several things:

- What makes the top performing women of the home-based business industry tick?
- Why are some women so incredibly successful in their chosen home-based business and others aren't?
- What kinds of families did they come from?
- Did birth order affect their success?
- Does their level of education make them more successful?
- What influenced their choice of companies?
- What kinds of books do they read?
- What type of music do they enjoy?
- What foods do they prefer?

Seventeen of the twenty-one women in the Women's Millionaire Club agreed to participate in the survey to help shed light on these questions. Their answers are listed anonymously, so that the respondents would feel comfortable providing candid answers.

I originally theorized that education, birth order and family would emerge as ingredients that led to these women's successes. Surprisingly, true patterns such as "first borns become millionaires," did not emerge. In fact, middle children were more prevalent, although not significantly.

The most decisive ingredient of success was self-development. Every woman in the club took complete control of their destiny by engaging in a rigorous self-development process. During a subsequent interview, Kathy Aaron referred to herself as a "self-development freak."

The following pages reveal the Women's Millionaire Club members' answers to my survey. Their responses provide an interesting glimpse into the life of a woman millionaire, and you'll see the Ingredients of Success that tie these powerful women together.

Snapshot: Women Millionaires

- We range in age from 29 to 69, but 70.6% of us consider ourselves Baby Boomers
- We are educated; 58.9% of us are college educated

- 94.9% of us in this study are Caucasian, but the industry is comprised of women of all colors, shapes, and sizes
- We came from families of all sizes. 5.9% were only children, 11.8% came from larger families and 35.5% came from middle-size families.
- Our birth order ranged from only child (5.9%) to first-born (29.4%), to middle child (41.2%), to youngest child (29.4%)
- Only one of us has never been married. The rest of us have been married at least once. As for multiple marriages, 41.2% have been married once, while 23.5% have been married twice, 11.8% have been married three times, and 5.9% have been married four times.
- When we do find the right person, we tend to stay married. 61.6% of us have been married for 10 or more years
- 82.3% of us have raised two to six children
- We're physically active. Our #1 activity is walking, but we also enjoy: cardio machines, free weights, sex, housework (yes, we do house work), swimming, cycling, tennis, hiking, golf, running, jogging and physical therapy. Half of us have physical trainers.
- Our health is important to us. 70.6% of us get a good nights' sleep and have healthy eating habits. We eat lots of veggies, little red meat, more chicken and fish, minimal breads and pastas. We try to avoid sweets and junk foods, and we take our dietary supplements every day.

- Before we became home-based business queens, we were stay at home mothers, teachers, real estate agents, models, secretaries, bookkeepers and CFOs. We worked in advertising, marketing, coaching, cosmetics, the mortgage industry, and even at IBM. We've done it all.
- Once we became home-based entrepreneurs, we took our work seriously. 82.6% of us work in our businesses full-time. (OK, so for some of us full-time means we work 20 hours a week, but we take those 20 hours seriously and accomplish a great deal)
- We explored different companies, but 29.4% of us got it right the first time and have been with that company ever since.
- The top five things that drew us to Network Marketing were: flexibility, additional income, compensation plans, work and life balance, and the mission and purpose of our organizations.
- We consider ourselves to be outstanding in the following areas: Ability to establish rapport (94.1%); viewed as a role model by others (94.1%); leadership skills (82.4%); communication skills (81.3%); ability to clarify information (76.5%), and product knowledge (70.6%). Please notice that these are all **learned skills.**
- We think we need improvement in the following areas: time management (29.4%); delegation (23.5%); continually sponsoring others (17.6%); follow-up skills (17.6%)
- We don't like to talk about money, but our net worths range from $1 million to $20 million. Forty-seven

percent of us make between $500,000 and $1 million per year.

- We are split right down the middle on having a coach versus not having a coach.
- We rank our priorities as follows: family, spirituality, making a difference, education, career, financial, tradition
- We consider our God-given talents to be anything from "Bridge Builder of People" to "Drawing out Other's Greatness." We love people.
- The one thing we all agree upon is the importance of self-development and personal development. 100% of us read about leadership, success, motivation, inspiration and spirituality each week. 70.6% of us listen to tapes, CDs or mp3s in these areas.
- 82.4% of us are always open to learning, 94.1% of us spend much of our time encouraging others to succeed and 70.6% of us are models for continuous improvement.
- We set goals that we write down, which give us a clear sense of purpose.
- One hundred percent of us attend our company's conferences and other industry conference. We all read our company's newsletters and other materials. We also read testimonials and other important information on our company's websites.
- ONE-HUNDRED PERCENT OF US WANT TO MAKE A DIFFERENCE!

The Survey Results

Education

What is your highest level of education?

Percent of Women	Education Level
17.6%	High School Graduate
23.5%	Some College
11.8%	College Graduate – Associate's Degree
35.3%	College Graduate – Bachelor's Degree
11.8%	College Graduate – Master's Degree

Age

The Women Millionaires in this study ranged from age 29 to 69. The majority are baby boomers between 44 and 63 years old.

Percent of Women	Years of Age
5.9%	18 – 29
23.5%	30 – 39
35.3%	50 – 59
35.3%	60 - 69

Ethnicity

What is your ethnicity?

Percent of Women	Ethnicity
5.9%	**Asian**
94.1%	**Caucasian**

Siblings

How many children were in your family?

Percent of Women	Number of Children in Family
5.9%	1 child
23.5%	2 children
35.5%	3 children
5.9%	4 children
17.6%	5 children
11.8%	7 children

Birth Order

What number child were you?

Percent of Women	Place in Family
5.9%	Only child
29.4%	First born
41.2%	Middle child
29.4%	Youngest

A Success Bite

Alfred Adler, an Austrian psychiatrist, was one of the original birth order theorists who noted the psychological situation of each child in the family is different, and may have an effect on personality development.

Adler theorized that:

- Only children like to be the center of adult attention, have difficulty sharing, prefer adult company, and like to use adult language.
- Oldest children can become authoritarian or strict, believe that power is their right, have high parental expectations placed upon them, and often are given early responsibility and are expected to set an example.
- Youngest children want to be bigger than others. They may have big plans that never seem to work out, are often spoiled, and can stay the 'baby' for years.
- Middle children are 'sandwiched' in and may be even-tempered, with a take it or leave it attitude. They can feel squeezed or have trouble finding a place, therefore they may become fighters of injustice.

Whether you are a first born, middle born, youngest, or only child, you can use your strengths to your advantage. The Women Millionaires did!

Family of Origin

What was your understanding of your family of origin?

Percent of Women	Family Type
5.9%	**Exceptional Family:** I wish everyone could have been in my family. The people who raised me had a rock-solid relationship and there was love and respect for all.
5.9%	**Average Family:** My family had its ups and downs, but there was love and respect for all. Everyone usually got along with a few bumps along the way.
52.9%	**Challenging Family:** One or both of the people who raised me had problems, which made living in our home challenging, to say the least.

Marital Status

What is your current marital status?

Percent of Women	Marital Status
5.9%	Single – never married
41.2%	Married once
23.5%	Divorced and single
29.4%	Divorced and re-married

How many times have you been married?

Percent of Women	Number of Marriages
5.9%	Zero – never been married
52.9%	Married once
23.5%	Married twice
11.8%	Married three times
5.9%	Married four times

If you are currently married, how many years have you been married?

Percent of Women	Length of Marriage
7.7%	1 to 5 years
15.4%	10 to 15 years
30.8%	15 to 20 years
7.7%	40 to 45 years
7.7%	45 to 50 years

A Success Bite

The majority of Women Millionaires were married only once, with an average of 15 plus years.

Ingredient of their Success ...
Stickability and Longevity

Which of the following best describes your spouse's employment status?

Percent of Women	Spouse's Employment Status
15.4%	Employed full time
7.7%	Not employed
7.7%	Stay at home spouse
23.1%	Works outside the home
23.1%	Works from home
53.8%	Self employed

How many children have you raised?

Percent of Women	Number of Children
5.9%	0 children
11.8%	1 child
35.3%	2 children
17.6%	3 children
5.9%	5 children
5.9%	6 children

How many children are living in your household?

Percent of Women	Children under 18 Living at Home
53.3%	0
8.3%	1
25%	2
8.3%	3

Percent of Women	Adult Children Living at Home
50%	0
16.7%	1
25%	2
8.3%	3

A Success Bite

Women Millionaires are Consummate Multi-Taskers

Studies have shown that females tend to be better than males at multi-tasking. In their book, *Why Men Never Remember and Women Never Forget,* Dr. Legato and Laura Tucker explain that women have more gray matter and more extensive communications between brain cells, especially in the frontal cortex (the area involved in judgment and decision making) They think that women may get more "brain bang for the buck" because of the greater connectivity between cells and greater blood flow.

Ruben and Raquel Gur, PhD's from the University of Pennsylvania, discovered that women, when given a variety of verbal or spatial tasks, use more parts of their brains, which may contribute to women's ability to focus on a number of different things at one time.

Physical Activities

Do you have a personal trainer?

Percent of Women	Response
41.2%	Yes
58.5%	No

What types of physical activities do you do daily or weekly? Responses listed by popularity:

- Walk (12 responses)
- Cardio machines (8 responses)
- Weights (8 responses)
- Sex (8 responses)
- House work (7 responses)
- Swimming (6 responses)
- Cycling (5 responses)
- Tennis (4 responses)
- Hiking (4 responses)
- Running (3 responses)
- Golf (2 responses)

- I'm thinking about

A Success Bite

... Get Moving!

All of the women millionaires do some form of physical activity.

The Centers for Disease Control and Prevention reports that regular physical activity, coupled with good nutrition, is important for overall good health.

getting physical
(2 responses)
- Jogging (1 response)
- Physical therapy (1 response)

Health

What is the average number of hour you sleep per night?

Percent of Women	Hours of Sleep per Night
5.9%	3 to 4 hours
23.5%	5 to 6 hours
70.6%	7 to 8 hours

What best describes your eating habits?

Percent of Women	Eating habits
11.8%	Extremely healthy – organic only
52.9%	Healthy eating habits
35.3%	Moderately healthy eating habits

Describe how frequently you eat the following foods/snacks:

Candy and Sweets

Percent of Women	Frequency
35.7%	Never touch it
35.7%	1 to 2 per week

Junk Food

Percent of Women	Frequency
35.7%	Never touch it
35.7%	1 to 2 per week

Drink Diet Soda

Percent of Women	Frequency
70.6%	Never touch it
17.6%	Daily
11.8%	1 to 2 per month

Drink Regular Soda

Percent of Women	Frequency
88.2%	Never touch it
5.9%	1 to 2 per week
5.9%	1 to 2 per month

Fruits and Veggies

Percent of Women	Frequency
5.9%	Addicted to it
41.2%	Daily
23.5%	1 to 2 per day
17.6%	3 to 4 per day
23.5%	4 to 5 per day
5.9%	1 to 2 per month

Red Meat

Percent of Women	Frequency
11.8%	Never touch it
5.9%	3 to 4 per day
41.2%	1 to 2 per week
11.8%	3 to 4 per week
35.3%	1 to 2 per month

Chicken and Fish

Percent of Women	Frequency
11.8%	Never touch it
17.6%	Daily
23.5%	1 to 2 per day
52.9%	3 to 4 per week
5.9%	1 to 2 per month

Breads, Rice and Pasta

Percent of Women	Frequency
6.3%	Never touch it
12.5%	Daily
6.3%	1 to 2 per day
37.5%	1 to 2 per week
18.8%	1 to 2 per month
18.8%	1 to 2 per month

Fast Food

Percent of Women	Frequency
43.8%	Never
18.8%	Weekly – once per week
6.3%	Weekly – twice per week
25%	Monthly – twice per month
6.3%	Monthly – three or more times per month

Take Dietary Supplements

Percent of Women	Frequency
5.9%	Never touch it
82.4%	Daily
11.8%	1 to 2 per day
5.9%	3 to 4 per week

Are you healthy (free from disease) or have you experienced illness, disease, or long-term disability?

Percent of Women	Frequency
41.2%	Very healthy
47.1%	Healthy
23.5%	Experienced illness in the past
5.9%	Currently experiencing illness

A Success Bite
... Get the Proper Rest to be a Success

The National Sleep Foundation says eight to nine hour of sleep each night is optimal for adults. The benefits of sufficient sleep include: alertness, memory and problem solving, and better overall health. Proper sleeping habits also reduce the risk of accidents.

The University Of Pennsylvania Medicine conducted a 2003 study, which reveals that cognitive performance declines with fewer than eight hours of sleep.

The Women Millionaires get plenty of rest, eat their veggies, minimize their consumption of red meat, soda pop, and fast food, and they TAKE THEIR DAILY NUTRITIONAL SUPPLEMENTS! They take their health seriously, and so should you!

Employment Status – Career
What was your work experience prior to becoming a Network Marketing Queen?

- Teacher
- Teacher, realtor, insurance agent, and computer programmer
- Teacher, business owner

- Teacher, stay at home mom, kinesiology and energy work, sponsoring courses
- Real estate
- Real estate agent
- I sold new homes and worked for a computer company in sales
- Modeling, executive secretary, podiatry assistant, real estate, mother
- Bookkeeper, financial manager, CFO
- Interior designer, and franchise restaurants owner – Burger King, Sizzler, and El Pollo Loco
- Advertising, marketing, coaching
- Architectural interior designer
- Cosmetic buyer, mortgage industry
- Worked in middle management for IBM
- Swimming coach
- Did charity work and raised my family
- Mom, events coordinator, graphic design

Which of the following best describes your current employment status?

Percent of Women	Employment Status
82.6%	Work from home, full-time for 20 hours or more per week (network marketing only)
11.8%	Employed part time in network marketing
5.9%	Works outside the home in another job, in addition to network marketing

A Success Bite

... Flexibility

Even though many of the women millionaires desperately needed money at the beginning of their careers, the single most important factor was flexibility.

Flexibility is a whole way of thinking and working ... it's all about choice. A new way to adapt the hours you work to balance your lifestyle and your family. You decide whether to work full time or less than full time.

Flexibility gives you the freedom to work where you want to work – home, the office, the park or the beach. Flexibility provides more autonomy about how you work. You figure out the best way to get the job done. You have the ability to customize your career path – to take time out or slow your pace. You decide whether it takes you one year or ten years to achieve your destination on your career path.

Flexibility is the new 'normal' for the Women Millionaires.

The person who is the most flexible controls of the situation.

How long have you been in network marketing?

Percent of Women	Number of Years
5.9%	3 years
5.9%	4 years
11.8%	5 years
5.9%	7 years
5.9%	9 years
11.8%	12 years
5.9%	13 years
5.9%	15 years
5.9%	16 years
5.9%	17 years
5.9%	18 years
5.9%	19 years
5.9%	25 years
5.9%	27 years
5.9%	30 years

How many network-marketing companies have you been involved with your career?

Percent of Women	Number of Companies
29.4%	1
23.5%	2
17.6%	3
11.8%	5
5.9%	7
5.9%	8
5.9%	10

A Success Bite

... Take YOUR Home-Based Business Seriously!

The length of time each woman spent in her home-based business varied, and many of the women explored several companies before settling into one company. The common thread ... the women millionaires all took their home-based businesses seriously and ran them like a business! To become a Top Performer, be CEO of your home-based business.

What were the most important features that originally attracted you to network marketing? (Responses listed in order of priority)

- Flexibility
- Additional income
- The money/compensation plan
- Work/life balance
- The organization's mission and purpose
- Empowerment and control
- Skill development and training opportunities
- Challenging and interesting work
- Organizational success and stability
- Retirement benefits
- Rewards and recognition

- Organizational culture
- Job security
- Career advancement
- Technology and tools
- Company benefits (i.e. trips, jewelry, cash bonus)
- Discounted/wholesale/free products

Income from Home-Based Business

Which range includes your highest one-year income?

Percent of Women	Income Range
35.3%	$300,000 to $500,000
47.1%	$500,000 to $1 million
5.9%	$1 million to $2 million
5.9%	$2 million to $3 million
5.9%	$3 million to $4 million

Which of the following ranges includes your approximate net worth?

Percent of Women	Net Worth Range
52.9%	$1 million to $2 million
11.8%	$2 million to $3 million
11.8%	$3 million to $4 million
5.9%	$4 million to $5 million
5.9%	$5 million to $6 million
5.9%	$10 to $20 million
5.9%	$20 million or more

Self Development

In regards to your home-based business, rate yourself:

Topic	Needs Improvement	Average	Outstanding
Product knowledge		29.4%	70.6%
Communication skills		18.8%	81.3%
Ability to establish rapport		5.9%	94.1%
Ability to ask open-ended questions		35.3%	64.7%
Ability to clarify information		23.5%	76.5%
Follow-up skills	17.6%	47.1%	35.3%
Responsive to requests for support or guidance	5.9%	29.4%	64.7%
Ability to respond to change		41.2%	58.8%
Time management	29.4%	58.8%	11.8%
Leadership skills		23.5%	82.4%
Sponsors others	17.6%	35.3%	47.1%
Coaches and develops team members	5.9%	47.1%	52.9%
Delegates	23.5%	47.1%	23.5%
Viewed as a model leader		11.8%	94.1%
Ability to duplicate		70.6%	29.4%
Makes touch choices		31.3%	68.8%
Shows respect for all team members		29.4%	70.6%
Catches people doing things right		52.9%	47.1%

Coaching
Do you have a coach?

52.9% of the Women Millionaires said that they did have a coach, citing these reasons:
- I need a role model
- It's encouraging, helps me to build skills, and allows me to learn who I am
- It is important to grow no matter what stage of life or business you are in
- Learning is a continual process. Everyone needs a coach to excel at their profession.
- I learn from my mentors and coaches who have achieved great success from ordinary circumstances. I am fascinated by learning their will, drive, skills and talents.
- I can never say I know it all; mentoring promotes growth and makes me accountable when I don't feel at my peak.
- I have a personal business and life coach as well as a personal trainer. I believe in learning.
- I need my coach's support and insight to be challenged and to grow.
- I need a coach to keep me on track, hear me vent, and hold me accountable.
- I have had a coach in the past and experienced great results. I felt the coaching was important because she helped me to learn to be more efficient with my time and more effective with people.

52.9% of the Women Millionaires said that they did NOT have a coach, citing these reasons:

- I just haven't explored this path yet.
- I am extremely self-motivated and "intention" directed, and believe that the through the books, tapes, and seminars I attend, along with my faith and beliefs, I have the greatest coach of all! He is forever opening doors, providing abundance in my life, and giving me the opportunity to serve others.
- I am happy with who I am.
- Most of the coaches are not in a more advanced place than I am, in life or business, and I cannot see how someone can coach me to get somewhere they are not!
- I'm self-sufficient, a quick learner, and if I ever felt as if I needed a coach, I would seek one out. I spend my days coaching others.
- Travel commitments prevent me from having a coach.
- No, I don't have a coach … but I am both a business coach and life coach to many others.

Rate yourself in the following personal development areas:

Topic	Seldom	Frequently	Always
Open to learning		17.6%	82.4%
Embrace change	5.9%	64.7%	29.4%
Involved in company activities and events	5.9%	11.8%	82.4%
Actions and behaviors consistent with words		41.2%	64.7%
Role model for constant improvement		29.4%	70.6%
Use 'coach' management style	5.9%	47.1%	47.1%
Use 'boss' management style	52.9%	11.8%	
Provides clear sense of purpose for team		35.3%	64.7%
Deals with issues in a timely manner		52.9%	47.1%
Listens effectively		58.8%	41.2%
Encourages others to succeed		5.9%	94.1%
Open to constructive feedback		52.9%	47.1%
Deals with conflict effectively	5.9%	58.8%	35.3%
Sets goals		47.1%	52.9%
Writes goals down	5.9%	41.2%	52.9%
Recognizes and rewards team members	5.9%	29.4%	64.7%

Reading
100% of the Women Millionaires read every week.

Listening to Tapes/CDs/Ipods
70.6% of the Women Millionaires use listening devices to learn each week.

Who are your favorite authors? (Responses listed in order of popularity)
- John Maxwell
- Wayne Dyer
- Robert and Kim Kiyosaki
- Napoleon Hill
- Dr. Tom Barrett
- Michael Clouse
- Caroline Myss
- Jack Canfield
- T. Hary Eker
- Steven Covey
- Jim Rohn
- Harvey Diamond
- Kevin Troudeau
- Martin Rossman
- Barry Bond
- Michael Gerber
- Martha Lowry
- John Milton Fogg
- Mark Yarnell
- Marianne Williamson
- James F. Twyman

- Robert Ohotto
- David Bach
- Og Mandino
- Brian Tracy
- Jodi Picoult/Sara Gruen
- J.D. Robb
- Mary Higgins Clark
- W. Clement Stone
- Frances Roberts
- TD Jakes
- Chris Widener

What are the topics/titles of your favorite books? (Responses listed in order of popularity)
- Bible, devotionals, and spiritual books
- Success-oriented books by personal development authors
- Books on health, nutrition, and science
- Autobiographies of strong women and men
- Leadership books
- Any millionaire books, such as *Secrets of the Millionaire Mind* and *Success of the Millionaire Mind*
- Og Mandino's *The World's Greatest Salesman*
- Network marketing and home-based business books
- Parenting books
- Fiction and science fiction
- Historic novels
- Mysteries
- Dog stories, such as *Marley and Me*

- Mary Higgins Clark books and other juicy mystery stories
- Books by John Grisham
- Books by JD Robb
- *Learning about Business One Story at a Time*
- Crime books
- Visualization books
- Self-development books

What are the titles of your favorite books? (Responses listed in order of popularity)
- *Rich Dad, Poor Dad*
- *Think and Grow Rich*
- *Power of Intention*
- *Anatomy of the Spirit*
- *Wisdom of the Tao*
- *Moses Code*
- *The Tipping Point*
- *Dare to Dream*
- *Work to Win*
- *Being the Best You Can Be*
- *Slight Edge*
- *The Secret*
- *Ten Things I Learned from Bill Porter*
- *Believe and Achieve*
- *Harper Book of Quotations*
- *Smart Woman*
- *7 Habits of Successful People*
- *Change your Thoughts, Change your Life*
- *The Laws of Prosperity*

- *Quiet Talks With The Master*
- *Principle Centered Leadership*
- *Dare to Dream Work to Win*
- *Eat, Pray, Love!*

What are your favorite audio programs or music?
- All training and self-development programs
- Self-development training with Jim Rohn, Michael Clouse, or Dani Johnson
- John Maxwell, Trump and Kiyosaki, and my company's business CDs
- Michael Clouse's *Total Success Pack*, Brian Tracy, Jim Rohn, and John Maxwell
- Jim Rohn, Tony Robbins, The Secret
- Jim Rohn
- Wayne Dyer and Ester Hicks
- *Awaken the Giant Within, 25 Ways to Success,* or any tape that teaches people skills (specifically communication skills).
- *Entering the Castle, Change your Thoughts Change your Life, Intuitive Power, Fundamentals of Spiritual Alchemy*
- Soothing music to wind down
- Classical music
- The Eagles and James Taylor
- Country music, and news programs
- All kinds of music

What magazines do you read? (Responses listed in order of popularity)

- My company's magazine and publications
- *Networking Times*
- *Time*
- *Oprah*
- *Newsweek*
- *Reader's Digest*
- *Shape*
- *Success*
- *Natural Health*
- *Runner's World*
- *USA Today*
- *Prevention*
- *Nutrition, Science*
- *Business*
- *Your Business at Home*
- *MLM Watchdog*
- *Martha Stewart*
- *Money*
- Any publication featuring strong ethics, principles, beliefs, and success strategies
- Mindless stuff
- *Enquirer, Redbook, and Women's World*
- Real stories
- Non business magazines

94.1% of the Women Millionaires read their company's e-Newsletters. What other e-mail newsletters or materials do you read?
- Nexera (Clouse)
- Jim Rohn Ezines, Chopra's ezines

- I research other company's information to stay current
- Caroline Myss, Wayne Dyer, VOS
- Dr. Mercola because he has the latest health information and articles. I also enjoy Hay House Radio, Robert Ohtoo, and Caroline Myss
- E-zines created by distributor leaders within our industry
- Paul Meyer, John Maxwell, and Dr. Mercola
- Magic Wand newsletters (which I write)
- T. Harv Eker, Big Al, Michael Olivery
- Nexera e-news by Michael Clouse and Chris Widener's ezine
- Sales, success.com, Nightingale Conant, e-Natural Selling, Michael Oliver, and Networking University
- Joel Osteen, Michael Clouse, Kim Klaver, Networking Times, DSWA, Shad Helmstetter, and Michael Fournier
- Michael Clouse and Jim Rohn.
- I read the newspaper daily because I believe I need to stay in touch with the world for the benefit of my grandchildren. We are making the world that we will leave for them and I want it to be a nice one.

What websites do you actively participate in or consider helpful to your Network Marketing business?
- My company's websites
- Facebook
- Make the Difference Network, Hay House, Mercola, and Josh Groban's site

- Make the Difference Network and Facebook
- Health related Websites
- MLM Watch Dog, MLM-DRA, and Pub Med

Conferences

What conferences do you enjoy?

- I love my company conferences and all company events
- I attend our annual convention – and haven't missed one in 18 years. It is necessary to bring new people to the conventions so they can see the company firsthand and understand who we really are.
- I attend all company sponsored national conferences, and produce three conferences of my own each year. One of these events is for women only, and is a spiritual and business retreat.
- My company's sponsored events are so important to me that I haven't missed any yet.
- I am usually a speaker at our international conferences, which has contributed greatly to my personal growth and speaking abilities.
- I love and attend many spiritual retreats across the country including business expos, Tony Robbins, Jim Rohn, Brian Tracy events, and the Unlimited Power conference
- Women's empowerment conference
- T. Hary Eker/Millionaire Mind
- Millionaire Mind Intensive

What conferences have helped you?

- My company's conferences
- Martha Lowry
- Brian Tracy
- Jim Rohn
- Shat Helmstetter
- Chris Widener
- Mark Fournier
- Women's conference
- Celebrate your Life, I Can Do It, A4MI, and my company's events
- All conferences assist in personal and business growth
- They have all helped me in one way or another. I gain something and grow from each event.
- My company's annual events and leadership events. I attend many other conferences as we exhibit throughout the year. They have all helped.
- My company's great leadership, business, and health training
- My company's conferences have helped me in investment and personal growth
- My company's annual conventions have helped me the most

Why is it important to attend conferences?

- Company conferences give you the bigger picture and help create relationships. I've heard that not all people that go to conferences get rich, but all rich people go to conferences.
- I am a believer in constant and never-ending improvement. I'm always ready to take my personal life or business to the next level and believe that

positive, motivational environments are conducive to growth. We are on a journey and there are lessons to be learned, new perspectives to consider, and people to meet every step of the way.

- Conferences are important for the training, but also so that we can hear stories of others' successes and failures. We have an opportunity to meet the scientists, company founders, and other distributors. Conferences are a must! Businesses change after these trips, so it's important to attend!

- The conventions are especially important for new distributors because they enhance their belief in the company. Conferences are also a good way to rub elbows with the who's who. You learn to adjust your goals to something bigger, but still achievable. For the leaders, conferences are a way of getting to know those other leaders who are willing to help your people that happen to be in their town. Exchanging ideas helps the group as a whole, and this is what I find to be so much fun.

- You are part of the company so you need to attend company conferences

- To stay focused and understand what's going on

- Continual learning and meeting successful people

- You are motivated by the synergy of the group

- To assist in my personal and business growth. You gain knowledge, information, meet new people, connect with new relationships, and expand all aspects of yourself

- Conferences sharpen my skills and knowledge, keep me current in the industry, and heighten my motivation and confidence
- Conferences keep me in touch with my downline from around the world
- I am a constant student and love to learn from others who have good ideas
- Constant learning is not negotiable
- Company conferences help people to become a leader. Don't attend if you don't want to make money!
- I attend conferences to grow and learn as a person and as a leader
- I attend conferences to be surrounded by like-minded people and get my cup filled

Professional Organizations

What professional organizations do you belong to?
- My church, DSWA, and Lifetime Networker
- My church
- Young Life
- High School Football Club until recently
- Make the Difference Network
- Women's Leadership Network and the National Insurance and Financial Planner's Association
- EWGA, E-Women Marketing, Chamber of Commerce, BTS
- Fresno Women's Network, Wellness Connections, and Strong Women Live Well
- DSWA, ASPCA, NRA, Concerned Women of America

- Distributor Rights Association
- Chamber of Commerce, AZ Leadership Force
- I've dropped out of many organizations because I'm semi-retired, but I'm still on the board of the Senior Community Center
- I don't go to meetings anymore, but I was once very active in Toastmasters and was also the charter president for the South San Francisco Jaycees

What events do you believe it's important to attend?
- My church services
- Charity events
- All company conferences
- Fund raisers for children's organizations and the San Diego Zoo
- Make the Difference Network, the Educational Kinesiology Foundation, and my company's and community events
- Non-profit organizations which we support
- Community and networking events are important to stay connected to the community and demonstrate that you are a professional providing valuable services
- Any event where you can make new friends and help your community
- All company conferences and Learn to Earn training seminars
- Any event that raises money for the poor, especially children
- Fundraisers for our children's private schools, crisis pregnancy centers, and Young Life

Why did you choose to get involved with the organizations you belong to?

- It's a way to serve mankind
- Connection, enrichment, and fellowship
- To meet others and give back to the community
- Children related
- Fullness of life
- I chose the San Diego Zoo because my husband was on the board. I chose the Senior Community Center because most people want to help the kids, but no one wants to help the older people who are desperate for our help. Most of the seniors at the community center would be on the street without our help.
- I want to support my son's activities
- Education, connecting with community and people, and giving back
- I have a passion for their purpose and love to support these causes
- I believe in the advancement and recognition of women doing well and wish to be active in my community.
- I went to many organizations to narrow it down to just a few. You can spend your whole day attending meetings and not doing your business. The organizations I've chosen work for me because they are social and/or networking business friendly
- They are helpful in the building and maintaining of my business

- They help me to learn and learning is constant growing
- These are important organizations that greatly affect our youth
- I want to leave a legacy

A Success Bite

... Learned Skills and Abilities

For far too long, the battle cry of upper management in corporate America has been first take care of your shareholders, second take care of the products and services, and if anything is left over, take care of your people.

The Women Millionaires have surpassed the corporations by following the principles of Servant Leadership. They have reversed the order of importance and have decided to take care of their people first. They have learned leadership and communication skills through intense self-development. Their incomes reflect that servant leadership pays!

Personal Information

What are your biggest priorities? Responses are listed in order of importance:

- Family
- Spirituality
- Making a difference
- Education
- Career
- Financial
- Tradition

Are you a big picture person or a more structured detail person?

87.5%	Big Picture Person
12.5%	Structured Detail Person

Are you more task-oriented or people-oriented?

35.3%	Task Oriented
12.5%	People Oriented

Do you tend to worry about things or accept obstacles as they come?

6.3%	Worry
93.8%	Accept

Describe your energy level.

5.9%	Energizer Bunny
70.6%	High Energy
23.5%	Medium Energy

What makes you laugh?

- A great comedy; my friends
- I'm not supposed to laugh at this, but people who are silly and don't know it!
- Seeing successes by my son and team
- My son: I think he is Jim Carey's spawn
- Children, fun activities, success, goofing around, sporting activities
- My grandchildren and people who have done well from both a health and wealth perspective
- Brilliant, funny people who possess quick, witty humor … and people who love to have fun!
- Funny stories, movies, my grandchildren, life experiences, and myself
- My friends and my granddaughter. I try to laugh a lot!

- A good book, my boy's stories, my son's dog, ridiculous things that my customers and clients say and do, and telemarketers
- My children, my dogs, silly movies, observing things that are silly, watching people's lives change or the better, babies, and little children
- Watching my grandchildren
- My son Jesse, a clean comedy act, the candid ways of little children, or a great joke about how men and women react to one another
- I laugh a lot. I think life is funny and people are funny – and I'm funny!
- Winning contests
- Doing enjoyable activities with family and friends
- My son, my husband, and my sister

What makes you cry?
- When a distributor with tremendous talent quits, or when one of my children or grandchildren are hurting
- Death and watching other people's lives change for the better
- Babies being born, weddings, and funerals
- Suffering by the elderly in life's changing events
- When someone I love hurts
- Births, marriages, and deaths
- Seeing the devastation in areas of the world that need so much care and attention ... especially the suffering children
- People who are struggling and won't look at the potential because of health issues or money issues

- Injustice, sorrow, and the pain of others
- Sad movies and pain in others' lives. I tear up a lot; even the news makes me tear up.
- Sad news and pain
- A good book, a sad movie, rejection, and being misunderstood
- My children, my dogs, tender, true stories, when people are kind to me, when loved ones suffer, and when people are cruel, liars, or cheaters
- Someone suffering from pain or financial disease
- Any sad movie, a hungry child, the loss of a loved one, an abandoned elderly person, or a misunderstood person, especially the ones suffering from mental disorders
- Suffering that others are enduring

Personal Presentation

How attentive to grooming and self-presentation are you?

Percent of Women	Rating
29.4%	Extremely attentive – I never leave my house without being dressed properly, with make-up applied
70.6%	Average attentive – I like to look good, but occasionally go out of my house in sweats and no make-up
0%	Not very attentive – I'm neat and clean but do not fuss very much over my appearance

A Success Bite

... Acceptance

The Women Millionaires have average concerns about their appearance, even though they are in the business of dealing with the public. These women know it's important to look good on the outside, but just as important (if not more!) to feel good on the inside. The Women Millionaires demonstrated a real ease with who they are as people and leaders.

The Women Millionaires came to acceptance by becoming aware of who they were. Because they accept themselves, they were better able to accept others. They learned to accept the people on their teams, wherever they were on their success journey, and are always encouraging and empowering their teams to move to the next level of awareness.

Why is self-presentation important (or not important) to you?

First Impressions
- Because I represent a health-oriented company, it's very important that I look the part. I keep my weight down, my attitude up, and my outlook youthful!

- First impressions are very important. You have to look successful to attract what you want.
- You only have one chance to make a first impression.
- You never know who you will meet and you only have one chance to make a first impression. I will occasionally go out to the mall in sweats, but not if I'm going to be in a place where I have the ability to talk to people or meet anyone in my organization.
- I have always believed that first impressions are important, especially in business. It is hard to convince others that you are successful when you don't look the part. In Network Marketing, you often only get one chance to convince another person that he or she can achieve success in a business venture. The other person has to be able to respect you not only for what you know, but for how you present yourself.
- Image is everything! Looking professional reflects on who you are and what you do.
- Attraction is an important part of this business. People look at us and think, "Do I want to be like them?" No one wants to look like a slob, yet I think people want to be themselves and not feel they are always "on." This is why I am fine with being in sweats and a ball cap when it's appropriate. I think that can be attractive, too.
- I believe most people judge you initially on your outward appearance, and believe we should always put our best out there. I am a professional and therefore, dress as one any time I am in a business

environment. Montana is a very casual place to live, so it is not uncommon to run into others when you are not dressed professionally, and it is more acceptable than in most areas of the country. I try to pay attention to my appearance, as I realize my identity is linked to my company, and I want to leave a positive impression in the marketplace.

- In business, I present myself as very classy and professional all the time. I love fashion and have fun being stylish. If I'm casually going out, (i.e. shopping, workout or travel) I still like to look good but enjoy feeling comfortable.
- Because people are always watching us, especially as leaders

To Feel Good About Me

- It's important that I feel good about myself and present myself to others as put together. I try to look professional. It's a habit for me. Also, I want to be pleasant looking for my husband. I believe that you dress the same inside your home as you do outside your home just as you eat the same inside your home as you do outside your home.
- I feel better when I am at my best. This allows me to be all I can be.
- I like to look my best, but don't get too worked up if I'm more casual or not wearing makeup. I think I look pretty good for a 50-year-old grandma!

- I feel better when I'm freshly showered, wearing clean clothes, and have my hair brushed and make up on. I do it for me.
- Whether we like it or not, people evaluate what we have to say by our personal presentation. It is also important to me to feel good about myself.

Talents

What is your special aptitude or God-given talent?

- Decorating
- Organizer (although I'm not organized myself!), and teaching and serving others
- To "get" things the first time around!
- I have a knack for training people in a way that is down to earth and more 'how to' rather than inspirational
- I am a natural teacher and love to support individuals in their personal growth and achievements
- I was blessed to have the ability to play piano by ear at the age of 4. At 15 years old, I was qualified to teach piano. I was a very talented dancer (jazz, tap and ballet). I began teaching at 12 years old, and went professional at 14 years old while studying in New York and L.A. Design, art and other creative work comes very naturally to me. Without previous art training, I graduated from design school with a 4.0 GPA. I have a natural ability to inspire people, assess their current situation and draw out their greatness. I have a photographic memory. I never get lost because I have an internal compass. I have intuitive

abilities that help toward current situations or future events.

- I can take someone's idea and make it happen. I am an administrator and know how to build teams to make things happen.
- I am a bridge-builder and a strong communicator, with a deep love of people of all kinds. I have the ability to bring people from many cultures, religions and backgrounds together to work and play in harmony. I am able to look at things from many perspectives, and have been called "Solomon" by many. I am intuitive, and use that gift when working with others to be sensitive to their needs and provide coaching and support when needed. I see the best in everything and everybody, which makes life easy for me. I always believe that things happen for a reason, and it serves me. I live life on-purpose, rather than accidentally (most of the time) and teach others how to do the same. That, I believe, is my gift.
- I have the ability to make people feel comfortable and at ease where ever I am.
- I am very adept at creating and sustaining systems for business. Organization comes naturally to me, and productivity is a natural outcome of good systems and organization. Marketing is something that creates a spark in me, and I love to teach on this topic. Connecting all the dots is fun, fun, fun!
- I am a good writer. I have a very compassionate and understanding heart. I seem to sense what people need or if they are hurting without them ever telling

me. I am good with children and animals. I am patient, truthful and sincere.

- I have a special talent for communicating and trying to listen to what people are saying and what they really mean.
- I am intuitive and have a strong sense of people. I have mastered the art of listening not only to people's speech, but also to their body language. I am witty and possess strong communication skills. Most importantly of all, I truly love people enjoy every minute of my experience with them.
- I have been given a gift to empathize - to feel what others feel. I have also been given a gift of painting a positive picture and motivating people to act.
- I have an ability to listen to people and be understanding. I help others achieve success.
- I am very sensitive to the will of God in my life, and am grateful for the gifts he's placed in my care. I give all the glory to God. I am empathetic, sincere, hard working and honest.

Note: Not all questions were answered by all participants. 'No response' was a selection on the survey.

A Success Bite

Self-Development is Essential for Success!

"Heaven helps those who help themselves."

The Women Millionaires take **responsibility for their success.** They are open to learning and spend much of their time on education. These women are addicted to learning and improving themselves. They took a practical look at their skills, and decided which skills they needed to improve upon to move their businesses forward. If they didn't know something, they sought a coach or mentor, either in physical form or through books and audio tapes. These women did not leave their success to luck, chance, or another person. They took full responsibility for their life!

"The willingness to accept responsibility for one's own life is the source from which self-respect springs."
-Joan Didion, American Journalist & Novelist

5 – The Women's Millionaire Club Behavioral Traits and Energy Profile

Have you ever wondered what makes women millionaires so successful? For the first time ever, this chapter will look at the women millionaire's success by assessing their personality profiles. Specifically, we will look at their **learned** behavioral traits, energy levels and energy styles as revealed by the ProScan® Survey by Professional DynaMetric Programs (PDP®).

Never before have women from various home-based businesses been surveyed, assessed and interviewed to this extent. The Gift of Possibilities these top performing women give you is their secret success profile. If you decide to make your own adjustments and develop these behavioral traits and energy styles, the impossible will become possible.

The "Hunter" Mentality in Corporate America

Before I met the members of the Women's Millionaire Club, I confess that I pre-judged all network marketing women as pushy and aggressive. Come on, fess up – you did, too. My judgment was clouded by my previous experiences in the corporate world. I

> # A Success Bite
>
> Behavioral traits and energy styles are learned!
>
> The Impossible, Becomes Possible!

assumed that these women would be similar to some of the corporate "hunters" I had worked with in traditional business.

In my experience, when a corporate "hunter" saw a prospect, they cornered, stalked, convinced and pressured the person to buy the product. Once the prospect said "yes," the hunter went in for the kill. He "tagged 'em" and "bagged 'em" by sending a completed application to the company as a prize trophy. When the customer was enrolled as a legitimate paying client, the hunter moved on to the next victim.

The Chase

People who display the "hunter" mentality often love the chase. They excitedly corner the client to purchase the product or stalk them until they enroll with the company. The corporate hunters try to convince the client to purchase and then apply strong-armed pressure to close the deal. This chase causes the client to push away and run even faster the other way or purchase with buyer's remorse.

The Catch

In the corporate world, the seller with the "hunter" mindset seems desperate to "catch" a prospect. The client senses desperation and bolts as soon as possible. If the "hunter" comes up empty, they make excuses and blame others.

Some of their self-defeating thoughts include:

- I don't have support from my family or my manager.
- I have poor management.
- My clients simply don't understand.
- I didn't receive enough training.
- The economy is crashing.
- Gas prices are too high.
- I don't have business cards or pamphlets.

The Results of the "Hunter" Mentality

The corporate "hunter" often feels discouraged and frustrated. When they move up to management, they lead with a 'demand and command' style. They tend to demand loyalty, shouting, "I'm the boss. You work for me!"

The "Farmer" Mentality in Network Marketing

When I began my research into network marketing, I believed that the women in the industry would exhibit the same "hunter" qualities I had observed in many corporate managers. My assumptions turned out to be incredibly wrong. In fact, these women display the opposite traits as corporate "hunters." They lead volunteer armies instead of paid sales forces, so they have learned to inspire others with their compassion and kindness.

The "farmer" mentality is a better representation of the women in network marketing. The farmer selects the seeds that will yield the best results. Then, the farmer creates an environment of growth. They sow the seeds, add nutrients to the field and water the plants. To cultivate the crops, the farmer needs to follow these steps in a specific order.

The Growth

The home-based business entrepreneur with the "farmer" mentality focuses on building relationships and nurturing others in the following ways:

> • Like a farmer prepares crops, the entrepreneur prepares the client by helping them clarify their needs and values. In other words, they help others discover their WHYs.
> • Farmers sow seeds, and entrepreneurs help clients outline their goals and aspirations in a similar way.
> • Entrepreneurs carefully select effective businesspeople to join in their business endeavor like a farmer sorts and selects seeds.
> • Farmers produce crops, and entrepreneurs with a "farming" mentality produce happy customers and valuable business builders.

Farmers Take Responsibility

If a farmer faces a natural disaster, they take responsibility and restore their land. Similarly, "farmers" in network marketing may need to rebuild their businesses. Instead of blaming others, they:

> • Have confidence that network marketing works.
> • Believe that they can and will reach the top.

- Take calculated risks to improve their businesses.
- Invite others to join their businesses.
- Learn everything they can to increase business.
- Understand that time and hard work is needed to build a solid foundation for a business.
- Treat their clients with respect and admiration.
- TAKE ACTION.

If an entrepreneur with a "farmer" mindset does not succeed, then they take responsibility to go back to the basics. They develop themselves by reading and listening to tapes in order to learn the skills necessary for success.

The Results of the "Farming" Mentality

Entrepreneurs with the "farming" mentality usually see steady growth in a lucrative business. The women in the Women's Millionaire Club possess the behavioral traits of an excellent farmer. They know how to **prepare, select, nurture and grow.** Alert – if you have a "hunter" mentality, network marketing is not the place for you. Those with a "farmer" mentality or a strong desire to learn a "farmer" mentality have a lot of potential to build a successful home-based business.

> **A Success Bite**
>
> To build a successful home-based business, become an excellent "farmer."
> **Prepare, Select, Nurture, and Grow.**

The Assessment

Although I have used various behavioral assessments in the past, I chose the ProScan® Survey by Professional DynaMetric Programs (PDP®) for numerous reasons. First, this one-of-a-kind assessment measures both behavioral traits and energy – the amount of energy one uses in accomplishing tasks and goals plus the levels of energy expended. Second, this assessment tests one's strengths and "aids in developing better communications, leadership, understanding and mutual respect." These positive attributes can help improve one's abilities in a home-based business. Last, this assessment is extremely accurate. Based on over 3.5 million responses, it uses extensive research and numerous case studies to compile a statistically based cross section of workers.

Behavioral Traits versus Temperament Types

From a psychological perspective, "temperament types" are innate aspects of a person's personality. They are genetically based, so you have these temperament types from birth. For example, an introvert and an extrovert are temperament types. The extrovert feels energized by social interactions, whereas the introvert feels energized by alone time. Temperament types cannot be learned or duplicated, since they are genetic predispositions.

Behavioral traits, on the other hand, are **learned** over time. They can be acquired with effort, coaching and a consistent self-development plan. These traits are based on how the individual perceives, feels, believes, or how one acts. In other words, the way you walk, talk, work, shop, drive and play. For example, a behavioral trait is extroversion. This measures one's ability to promote their ideas verbally to influence others. One can learn to speak more effectively by improving verbal skills.

My focus centered on behavioral traits for two reasons: they can be acquired and they influence a majority of our actions. All people have one behavioral trait that seems to rule our personalities, called the Primary Behavioral Trait. This trait is comfortable for us to use, so 50-70% of our observable behavior is a result of this single trait. Although this trait can be changed or acquired, it takes a considerable amount of effort and energy.

A Success Bite

Temperament Type: Genetically based. An extrovert is a person energized by spending time with people.

Behavioral Trait: <u>LEARNED</u> Extroversion is the learned ability to verbally promote your ideas or influence others.

Duplicate the Success **Behavioral Traits** exhibited by these Top Performers to build a successful home-based business.

Remember: Behavioral Traits **can be Learned or Acquired**.

Behavioral Traits in Everyday Situations

Let's explore how behavioral traits can show up in an everyday scenario. Imagine waiting for an elevator. When the door finally opens, the elevator is crowded with people. The following four Primary Behavioral Traits determine how one acts in this scenario:

Dominance (the "Take Charge" Trait) – This trait determines how a person responds to problems and gets things done. A person with a primary dominance trait takes control of their environment through *things*. They would enter the elevator with determination, feeling confident that the elevator could hold one more person. Then, they would immediately control the buttons.

Extroversion (the "People" Trait) – This trait determines how a person verbally influences others. A person with the primary extroversion trait controls their environment through people. They would enter the elevator with a smile. Since they enjoy meeting people, they would be delighted at the sight of a packed elevator. Immediately, they would start chatting with people and gleefully say, "Isn't this cozy?"

Pace (the "Rate of Motion/Patience" Trait) – This trait determines the rate at which a person moves or adapts. A person with the primary pace trait controls their environment through process and are influenced by the environment. They would be taken aback by the number of people in the elevator. Therefore, they would move at a slower pace and would kindly say, "Please go ahead. I'll wait for the next elevator."

Conformity (the "Systems" Trait) – This trait determines how a person is influenced by the systems in their environment. A person with the primary conformity trait controls their environment through rules. They would feel more comfortable following the rules. Therefore, they would count the people in the elevator and check the posted maximum capacity before reluctantly entering the elevator.

The Cornerstone Behavioral Traits

The four important behavioral traits can be measured. A person with high dominance, for example, has different attributes than a person with low dominance. The women millionaires displayed the traits in the bolded boxes on the following page.

Dominance	Extroversion	Pace	Conformity
High Dominance direct, decisive, competitive. This person challenges authority and exerts control.	**High Extroversion articulate, enthusiastic, interactive, persuasive, influential. This person seeks opportunities, builds teams, and delegates tasks well.**	High Pace steady, consistent, persistent, dependable. This person is cautious of change. **Midline Pace flexible, adjustable**	High Conformity structured, accurate, loyal. This person follows and maintains established systems.
Low Dominance supportive, moderate, collaborative.	Low Extroversion contemplative, private, imaginative.	Low Pace spontaneous, versatile. This person is action-oriented and has a sense of urgency.	**Low Conformity independent. This person values personal freedom and minimal external controls.**

The Assessment Results

The Women's Millionaire Club members were unaware of their behavioral traits until after careful assessment when their behavioral success trends emerged. As Terry Anna, the exclusive PDP® consultant for the Women's Millionaire Club says, these women have "mastered the art of being nurturing 'farmers' with a touch of 'hunter' in them. They have capitalized on their ability to think 'outside-the-box' and to persuade others verbally to 'go-for-the-gusto' in life. They have an uncanny sense of intuition that allows them to pull from their knowledge and experiences quickly in various ways to promote their ideas. Because of their high energy levels, they are self-starters with a sense of inner direction. They tend to be comfortable with who they are and are perceived as authentic by others." (See appendix for contact information regarding PDP© assessment and Terry Anna.)

Extroversion – The People Trait

86% of the women in the Women Millionaire's Club display high extroversion traits. They like being around people and verbalize easily with others. They have learned to verbalize quite effectively and can engage in casual conversations

---

A Success Bite

The Women's Millionaire Club tend to be: articulate, enthusiastic, interactive, persuasive, and influential. They seek opportunities, build teams, and delegate technical tasks.

---

anywhere they go. These top-performing women charm others with their enthusiasm. The room seems to light up when they arrive, as they are often the "life of the party." They know how to train and develop others with encouragement and manage others well by creating strong support systems. They avoid or steer clear of negativism.

Dominance – The Take Charge Trait

While 57% of these successful women display low dominance traits naturally, 62% acquired their low dominance traits over time. Like most women, the women in the Women Millionaire's Club are collaborative and

---

A Success Bite

The Women's Millionaire Club tend to be: mild-mannered, composed, modest, and accommodating. They support others and collaborate to accomplish results. They also prefer not to impose demands upon others' time and work loads.

---

accommodating. They are supportive team members who enjoy including others in group projects. They are accepting and cooperative.

Conformity – The Systems Trait

These home-based business entrepreneurs greatly enjoy independence, are open-minded and seek freedom. 71% of them

---

A Success Bite

The Women's Millionaire Club tend to be: independent and uninhibited in style. They relate well to out of the ordinary activities, seek freedom with minimal control in all areas of life, and enjoy taking risks.

---

display low conformity qualities. While they have a healthy understanding of the standards in network marketing, they use the standards to pave their own paths. They prefer to ask for forgiveness rather than for permission.

Pace– The Rate of Motion Trait

53% of the women in the Women Millionaire's Club display a mid-line pace. This means that they are adaptable and

> ## A Success Bite
>
> The Women's Millionaire Club tend to be: adaptable, easy-going, amiable, versatile, and open to change.

can adjust their tempos to meet the demands of the situation. They exhibit a balance of patience and a sense of urgency. This mid-line pace also suggests an element of the "hunter" mentality, which promotes forward movement.

Behavioral Trait Pairs

Behavioral Trait Pairs are an exclusive component of this assessment. These behavioral pairs are two single traits that combine one strength over another strength. The women in the Women Millionaire's Club display behavioral trait pairs that give them a competitive edge in network marketing.

The Persuasive/Seller Trait Pair

The persuasive/seller trait pair reflects extroversion over dominance, meaning the extroversion is more pronounced in people with this trait pair. 91% of the women surveyed naturally exhibit this trait pair.

The persuasive/seller trait pair describes people who enjoy discussing and sharing ideas. They are also positive and optimistic. They show empathy toward others and place a high value on working as a team member. To accomplish a task, they elicit help in a friendly and persuasive way.

The Fast, Fluent Communications Trait Pair
The fast, fluent communications trait pair reflects high dominance over low pace. 52% of the women in the Women Millionaire's Club naturally display this trait pair. This means they have the ability to convey ideas quickly and effectively in a way that influences others. One important note is that 62% of the women did not have this trait pair naturally and developed these behaviors with practice.

Logic – How One Makes Decisions

This assessment uniquely measures logic, or the style one uses in making life decisions. Decisions are made based on three important elements:

1. Facts
A person who is analytical deliberately makes decisions based on the documented facts and the information provided.

2. Feelings

A person who is intuitive makes decisions based on their inner sense, their "gut feeling."

3. Balanced

A balanced person can use both facts and feelings to make decisions depending on the situation. They may use facts when information is required. They may use intuition when they must make a rapid decision or if facts are not available.

86% of the women in the Women Millionaire's Club are **intuitive decision makers**, compared to 60% of the general public. This intuition helps them in various ways. For example, they may be very knowledgeable about a company or a compensation plan, but they will most likely choose a company based on their intuition, or gut feeling. The numbers may appear accurate, yet these women won't make decisions unless it feels right.

Energy
Energy Styles

The ProScan® Survey by Professional DynaMetric Programs is the only assessment that measures energy – both energy styles and energy level.

Energy styles are how tasks are approached and goals are completed. Tasks can be approached in three main ways:

1. Thrust
This style is similar to launching a rocket. Thrust involves incredible inner direction, self-starting, and intense energy to accomplish a task.

2. Allegiance
This style is a supportive style dedicated to completing a project with a sense of connection with others and common purpose.

3. Ste-nacity (a coined PDP® term that combines "steady" and "tenacity")
This locomotive-like force is a persistence style that takes a steady and tenacious approach to a task.

The women in the Women Millionaire's Club mainly use the thrust style. In fact, 76% of the women were "goal rockets" who used thrust to accomplish tasks. 81% of the women in this group learned this style over time. This thrust is an element in the "hunter" mindset that keeps these women working hard towards a goal and promotes results. When these women started their businesses, tasks were their jet fuel that propelled them like laser rockets towards their written goals. They didn't need anyone to push them along; they were self-directed.

Nineteen percent of the women surveyed exhibited a back-up style, predominately the allegiance style of energy. Therefore, they used a supportive style and emphasized team unity. This is more true to the "farmer" mindset and is more often used when the thrust style cannot achieve the desired results.

Energy Level

Kinetic energy is the measurement of the mental, emotional and physical energy used to accomplish a task or attain a dream. Like the cells in a cellular phone, you either have a full charge and enough energy to complete a task or you must be recharged. The constant use of too much of one's natural energy level can be wearing. Rest, sleep, vacations, or a change in pace is sometimes necessary to restore your energy.

> ## A Success Bite
> ### Like Energy, Attracts Like Energy
>
> Three women, in the same "downline," rated in the highest Energy Level range – Ultra Force. They are often called "Energizer Bunnies on Steroids" -- they keep going, and going, and going.

These successful women have a higher energy level than the general public. On a scale of one to seven (one being the lowest energy level and seven being the highest energy level), most people average a four. 90% of these women, however, placed between four and seven. In fact, almost 30% are between levels six and seven. They actively move towards their goals with great energy. Even during their resting time, they think about their goals.

Energy Drain

Energy drain refers to the amount to which a person allows stress to affect their available energy. Energy drain is the net result of stress and satisfaction levels. When a person runs out of energy, three symptoms appear: an increased susceptibility to accidents, a decrease in effort and an attempt to escape the situation (through excuses, conflicts of commitment, or illness).

The women in the Women Millionaire's Club experience minimal energy drain. Over 71% exhibit a lower-than-normal energy drain. They manage stress well by taking frequent breaks and sleeping at least seven hours each night.

Authenticity

These successful women are often very comfortable in their own skin. They come across as authentic. If they are uncomfortable with some aspect of their personalities, they take steps to improve. These women refer to themselves as "Personal Development Junkies," because they continuously work on improving themselves.

Satisfaction

The assessment also measures each woman's satisfaction, or the level at which her personal needs are being fulfilled. The level of satisfaction often reflects whether or not the individual receives the proper rewards from their environment and whether their goals and aspirations are being met.

A high level of satisfaction indicates that the person's stress is worth the energy expended for the rewards they receive. Over 52% of the women assessed have a high level of satisfaction. They have high morale and feel satisfied with life. 29% of the women fall into the average level of satisfaction, which indicates that the person is coping well. The rewards are worth their efforts. The women millionaires tend to feel that the energy and effort they "put in" to their business was worth the rewards they received.

Assessment Snapshot: Women Millionaires

The following snapshot is a collection of the profiles displayed by the women millionaires.

- When in charge of people, we prefer to use a "farmer" style, which is more friendly, empathetic and persuasive (a persuasive/seller trait pair).
- We have the ability to convey our ideas and influence others in a quick and effective manner (fast, fluent communications trait pair).
- We appreciate self-confidence and independence. (seeks change/innovative trait pair)
- We are willing to take calculated risks to reach our goals.
- We seek freedom as opposed to being tied to tradition. We detest unnecessary rules and regulations and may even ignore them. (low conformity)

- We are somewhat competitive and ambitious. Each time our company has a contest, to earn a reward we desire, we will earn it. (touch of the 'hunter' style)
- When we are in charge, we are supportive, moderate, and collaborative (low dominance).
- With respect to our relationships, we are enthusiastic, interactive, persuasive and influential.
- We seek opportunities, build teams and delegate tasks (high extroversion).
- We are flexible and versatile. We can act with a sense of urgency to get results (mid-line pace).
- We value our freedom and prefer minimal external controls (low conformity).
- Although we know the facts and figures, we tend to make decisions based on intuition and "gut" feeling (logic-intuitive).
- With us, what you see is what you get (authentic).
- We have intense energy and approach our tasks and goals like a rocket launch. We are self-directed and self-motivated (thrust energy style).
- We have high levels of mental, physical and emotional energy. We usually run out of time in the day before running out of energy (high kinetic energy).
- We can manage our stresses. We expend a lot of energy, so we are careful to take breaks and rest. Most of us sleep at least eight hours each night (low energy drain).

• We have a high degree of satisfaction because we feel that the energy we exert brings the rewards we desire (high satisfaction).

• The behavioral trait we use most often is our people trait (high extroversion).

The Importance of Behavioral Traits and Energy Styles

The best way for a person to achieve success in a home-based business is to assess one's own traits with the ProScan® Survey by Professional DynaMetric Programs (PDP®). The key is to identify the differences between yourself and successful millionaire women and then to map out a self development plan. (For more information on the assessment or self-development plan, see the Appendix).

Many women in network marketing had to push themselves to adapt to the world of network marketing. "I wasn't a light that people wanted to come to," Doni Smith says. "I had to learn to become a light." Because many of the traits necessary for network marketing are distinct from those in traditional businesses, many

---

A Success Bite

Success Behavioral Traits can be Learned or Acquired with:
- Time
- Effort
- A Self-Development Plan
- Mentoring and or Coaching

---

women must make adjustments. Brenda Loffredo admits, "I came from corporate IBM. I had to learn to be more of a people person." The good news is that, with time, consistent effort, a self-development program, mentoring, and coaching, these behavioral traits and energy styles **can be learned or acquired**.

The Secret Recipe For SUCCESS!

·KNOW WHAT YOU WANT.
Explore and clarify your thoughts.

·BELIEVE YOU CAN HAVE IT.
Examine and understand your beliefs and feelings.

·TAKE ACTION.
Learn to act appropriately and consistently.

·GIVE THANKS.
Appreciate your results.

6 – The First Ingredient: Know What You Want

The 2008 Beijing Olympics were electrifying. Viewers around the world collectively held their breath as a 41-year-old single mother named Dara Torres swam against athletes less than half of her age. By the age of 30, most swimmers assume their competitive swimming days are over. However, in her fifth Olympic attempt, Dara won two silver medals. Dara proudly gave her gift of possibilities to 70 million viewers.

Dara's gift was a lesson, "If I can do it, you can too. **Don't put an age on your dreams**." Suddenly, mature athletes around the world began training for another Olympic attempt. Dara's gift made the impossible possible.

The women I interviewed for this book graciously gave their gifts of possibilities to you. They exposed their recipes for success to help others succeed in a business that has unlimited possibilities – network marketing. Almost every woman expressed a desire to help others attain their same level of freedom and success. Their stories are examples of how everyday people can make the impossible possible.

Decision Time

The book you are holding is a gift of possibilities. To make a change in your life, decide right now. You have three options:

1. Ignore this gift, put the book on your bookshelf and continue on with your life.
2. Read this book and think, "That's nice for those women but I can't do what they did."
3. Rip the book open with reckless abandon and realize the limitless opportunities available to you.

The gift is in your hands.   The choice is yours.

The Success Gene

When I set out to write this book, my goal was to explore the qualities that made some women successful in their home-based businesses. I wondered whether or not these women millionaires had a "success gene" that gave them innate abilities over others. What I learned from the assessment and interviews was that these women were not born with any inherent gene for success – they **Learned to Succeed**.

In fact, the women millionaires come from all different backgrounds. Some came from supportive families, while others came from challenging families. Some came from successful business backgrounds, while others never had any business experience. Some were just starting out in network marketing, while others were on the verge of retirement. From my research, I concluded that there is no 'singular type' of background that will lead to success in network marketing.

Follow the Recipe for Success

If the secret to success is not genetic, what makes these women so successful? After researching and evaluating these women, I discovered that the key to success is in their patterns of behavior. The women all took a similar approach to network marketing.

A Success Bite

Success is not in the genes, it's in your Patterns!

Thoughts create **Beliefs** that precipitate **Action**. Repetition of the Thought, Belief and Action Patterns create a Habit. Change the patterns to change a habit.

Patterns are everywhere. Scientists look for patterns to find a cure. Athletes look for patterns to win competitions. Corporations look for patterns to gain a competitive edge. It's time for women to look at the patterns of behavior in the top performing women of home-based businesses. A pattern gives you the power to help form a recipe for success.

Each women millionaire had their own experiences, but they all used the same basic recipe for success with the same ingredients. Each woman enhanced the recipe by adding her own personal ingredients in varying amounts. To become a top performing millionaire, however, you must use all of the main ingredients.

Their Secret Main Ingredients for the Recipe for Success

- **KNOW WHAT YOU WANT.** Explore and clarify your thoughts.
- **BELIEVE YOU CAN HAVE IT.** Examine and understand your beliefs and feelings.
- **TAKE ACTION.** Learn to act appropriately and consistently.
- **GIVE THANKS.** Appreciate your results.

Thoughts: The Gift of Possibilities

Your mind is like a video camera. Every experience, both good and bad, is taken in, unedited, through your senses. Once you have captured the experience, you formulate concepts called "thoughts" about the information you received. Those thoughts, when combined together, form your image or picture of reality.

Thoughts can be extremely powerful, even when they are irrational. For example, as a teenager, I often saw popular kids and popular TV characters smoke. My mind took in these images. I formed the thought that "smoking makes a person popular." Based on that thought, I developed a belief that "I could be popular as well if I

> **A Success Bite**
>
> Thoughts form your Pictures of Reality.

smoked." Even though I chocked on my first cigarette, I pushed past the discomfort and developed a 20-year habit.

After adopting my daughter, Mayre, I could not seem to quit smoking, but I did decide never to smoke in front of her. For the longest time, she had no idea that I smoked. One night, I stepped outside to have a cigarette while Mayre was sleeping. She awoke in a panic, as she had forgotten to ask me to sign a permission slip for school. She came running outside with a paper in hand. When she saw me smoking, she stopped abruptly. Mayre started sobbing and cried, "My teacher says that people who smoke are going to die! If you die, who will take care of me?" My thoughts changed in an instant. I decided to stop smoking. I quit the habit for good.

How did I change so quickly? I **decided**! Decisions change our images of reality. A vividly clear picture flashed in my mind of my daughter all alone at my funeral. This picture allowed rapid access to the unconscious. Instantly, I knew exactly what I wanted – to quit smoking immediately.

A Success Bite

The unconscious mind has the power to control all of your important life decisions.

Thoughts on Network Marketing

The women millionaires I interviewed all had certain thoughts about the network marketing industry. Like many people, at first, most of them thought network marketing was a "scheme." The strength of these thoughts was based on a life experience. Even if the experience did not actually happen to them, they internalized someone else's experience and developed a picture about network marketing. The picture created either a positive or negative thought.

Regardless of their experiences, the women millionaires changed their thoughts about network marketing by refocusing and changing their internal images and changing their language.

When Carolyn Johnson's cousin introduced her to network marketing in 1970, her first thought was, "Isn't that what people do when they don't want to work or when they want to 'get rich quick?'" She kindly turned her cousin down and decided to "get a real job."

Many years later, Carolyn attended a family reunion and experienced her cousin's wealth with all of her senses. She saw his beautiful house, sat in his luxurious cars and heard his vacation stories. It changed her image of reality. "I decided to trust him and learn from him," she says. Her sensory experiences affected her thoughts. In her unconscious mind, Carolyn vividly imagined herself living that lifestyle. As a result, the mental picture she had of network marketing changed instantly. "It's not a scheme," she thought. "It's a legitimate, lucrative business opportunity." Her beliefs, and then her actions, changed.

Language Changes Reality

Language can change a person's beliefs and ultimately an entire nation. As a red-haired Irish woman, I have always been intrigued by Irish history. Irish history demonstrates the power of language. In 1831, Gaelic was the official language spoken by over 4 million people. That year, however, the British changed the official language to English. At first, the Irish upper class resisted the change. Over time, Gaelic was associated with poverty, famine, and peasantry. English became the language of success and commerce. In less than two generations, only 5% of the Irish population spoke Gaelic.

The British recognized a powerful truth – change the language and you change the culture. The same is true in network marketing. Change your language to change your image of reality. **All 100%** of the women millionaires used the word "**DECIDE**" as a main ingredient for success.

A Success Bite

'DECIDE' to change your language. Your picture of reality will change. Vivid new pictures allow rapid access to the unconscious.

The word "decide" can dramatically alter a person's life. This significant word comes from the Latin word "decidere," meaning "to cut off, cut the knot, determine." Each woman decided to determine her own destiny. Kathy Aaron was unhappy with her situation and needed a change: "I came home from a network marketing event and **decided** to join. I wanted a way out of real estate and into something with a residual income." Her new language transformed her picture of reality.

A Clear WHY

Language can change your mental images of network marketing. Your WHY is the language that sharpens your picture so it's crystal clear. Every woman millionaire had a clear WHY. "Family was WHY I started, and family is still my WHY," Barbara Freundt maintains. A clear WHY gave each top performer fortitude when faced with obstacles.

Men and women often have different WHYs because their images of reality differ. Men, for example, often picture themselves in sports cars with their wallets full of money. For women like Jodi Whittemore, other priorities are more important: "My WHY was so clear," she says. "I wanted the time freedom to be with my family and to enjoy vacations with each other." Women often formulate their WHYs based on family, faith and friends.

Knowing a person's WHY helps them set personal goals. Before the women millionaires asked a client to join the company, they asked about the person's needs, desires and goals (essentially, their WHY). "Discover WHY your clients want to do this business," Susan Walsh advises. "A vivid WHY is the key to success. If they do not have a crystal clear WHY, it's hard to help them." A person can only move forward in the business with a clear purpose in mind.

Imaginative questions help discover the person's true desire. A logical question, for example, may be, "Why do you want to start a home-based business?" This direct approach may provide information without insight. "I don't know...I guess I want more money." This does not tap into their unconscious images of reality or their true desire.

Use an imaginative approach to unleash the person's unconscious thoughts and desires. For example:

"Imagine you are wandering through an antique store. You accidentally bump into a table and knock over an ornately-designed, multi-colored bottle. It falls to the floor, but amazingly does not shatter. A mystical genie floats out of the bottle and says, 'I will grant you three wishes. What does your heart desire?'"

> # A Success Bite
>
> The Language we use
> Programs the Reality we
> Experience!

Imaginative questions help the person explore their unconscious desires. The genie enables the person to think of wishes that may not seem practical or realistic at the time. Tapping into the imagination helps the person revert back to childhood, a time when dreams and fantasies seemed more possible. This exercise is ultimately to discover what the person wants, which will help them build a more positive set of beliefs about network marketing. Only then can they truly realize the various possibilities available in the industry.

7 – The Second Ingredient: Believe You Can Have It

Beliefs

"Whether you believe you can, or you can't, you are right," said Henry Ford. Beliefs are what you hold to be 'certain truth' whether it is true or not.

Beliefs are formed through sensory experiences. The belief is strengthened when learned with intense feelings. Feelings hold the belief in place. By spending time with others who hold the same belief we create evidence for our beliefs.

A story from my childhood perfectly demonstrates how a belief is formed. The teacher asked me to name an animal that lays eggs. I proudly blurted out, "The Easter Bunny!" All of the children laughed, but I didn't see the humor in the statement at all. I had seen and talked to what I thought was the real Easter Bunny. The entire experience was full of joy and excitement for me, cementing my belief in the Easter Bunny. I also played with other children who believed in the Easter Bunny, which further supported my belief.

One Woman's Belief

One member of the Women Millionaire's Club, Susan Walsh, always thought she could "have it all." For years, she was told that she could achieve anything. She believed with absolute certainty that she could achieve anything and also have it all. She owned and managed a hair salon while raising two darling sons and spending time with her husband as well. She worked with other women who shared her belief system. However, the worked piled up, and soon Susan felt overwhelmed. She no longer had time to devote to her children or to her wonderful husband. She felt helpless.

Susan's picture of reality changed when her eldest son announced his acceptance into medical school. Although Susan was ecstatic, her heart sank at the same time. How would she cover the extra payments? Trading hours for dollars suddenly was not working for her. Her thoughts opened to the possibility of making money in another way. Susan was introduced to residual income.

When presented with this new information, a new picture of reality, and different language, she immediately changed her belief—'network marketing will work for me'. Her new belief resulted in new actions – Susan became teachable and made a different business plan.

A Success Bite
To change your Beliefs develop a New Picture of Reality, use different Language and Gain New Information through Self-Development.

Self-Development

To master network marketing become a Self-Development 'freak' advises Kathy Aaron. You must believe in the company and the products, but most importantly, you must believe in yourself. As author and entrepreneur Jim Rohn said, "Work harder on yourself than you do your business." The women millionaires did exactly that. They attended conferences, seminars, classes and coaching sessions. They did online training , read every book and magazine on the industry. They listened to CDs , MP3s and tapes. Over time, they gained a consistent stream of information that built and supported their beliefs.

In focusing on personal development, the women millionaires developed a belief in themselves. One of these women, Kathy Aaron, says, "Personal development is the cornerstone of success. It is the anchor. It's what keeps you on track. It's what brings you back on track if you get off track." These women built a strong belief in themselves. In doing so, they laid the emotional and mental foundation for their successes.

Spaced Repetition

Beliefs are typically collected from parents, teachers, friends, preachers and other influences in one's life. When I was raised, my mother reinforced positive statements in my mind. She repeatedly told my brother that he was great with his hands. As an adult, my brother worked as a plumber for the United States Air Force. My mother often exclaimed that my sister was great with numbers. My sister worked in Congressional Records in Washington, DC. My mother always said to me, "You are so funny. You are my MGM, my big production." Even though many people have a fear of public speaking, I grew up to be an international speaker. Words

> **A Success Bite**
>
> Read Maxwell Maltz's
> **_Psycho-Cybernetics_** to
> learn more about Spaced
> Repetition as a
> learning technique.

spoken at intermittent intervals can create belief over a period of time.

Spaced repetition can also influence your beliefs about yourself. Positive words that are spoken with kindness usually create positive beliefs. These enhance self-esteem. On the other hand, negative words that are spoken in anger usually create negative beliefs. These damage self-esteem.

Take Inventory of Your Beliefs

Chefs regularly take inventory. They check for needed items. Just like a master chef, you need to take inventory of your beliefs. Get rid of the beliefs that don't work. These negative beliefs will hold you back from reaching your goals.

One negative belief that held me back was the idea that the _rich get richer and the poor get poorer._ When I explored this belief, I discovered that rich people have different thoughts about money. They spend time with other rich people, learning investment strategies that I had never heard of. They make different financial choices. Instead of dwelling on my negative thoughts, I made the conscious decision to rethink what I had previously believed.

Take a close look at all of the areas in your life. Systematically review the beliefs that you hold regarding each area. Ask yourself whether or not each of the following beliefs is based on fact or opinion:

- Spiritual beliefs
- Family beliefs
- Relationship beliefs
- Career beliefs
- Money beliefs
- Time beliefs

How to Change Your Beliefs

To change your beliefs, first identify outdated or negative beliefs, make the decision to change them. Vividly create a new picture of how you would like your life to be. Change your language. Gain new information. "The more you learn, the faster you go," said Joyce Dell. Hang with people who already hold the beliefs you would like to have. The very fact that you are reading this book means you can incorporate new ideas into your belief system. The women millionaires surrounded themselves with positive people and embraced new habits. You can too!

Put Frosting on Your Beliefs

When you bake a cake, you mix the ingredients together and put the batter into the oven. Even though you may not be able to see the physical cake in the oven, you have faith that the cake will still be there when the timer rings. You believe in something you cannot see.

The Industry

Like many people, the women millionaires started with the false notion that network marketing was a 'scheme.' However, they educated themselves to strengthen their beliefs in network marketing.

Carolyn Johnson, an amazing woman millionaire, took the learning process very seriously: "I learned about the industry. No matter what you do in life, there is a learning curve. No business worth owning has just a two or three month learning curve. The network marketer has to study like a doctor if they want to be good at what they do. You have to learn everything you can about the industry. That's what I did to be successful." Carolyn's self-education enabled her to reach the highest levels of success.

Another incredible woman named Donna Johnson understands the benefits of education. She says, "For some reason, in our network marketing industry, if people get started and don't make big money right away, they quit and blame the industry. They never took the time to learn the real truth about network marketing. I think that, because it is so easy to get into this industry, it's easy to get out. I help people manage their expectations and really learn the industry, company and products, so they can hunker down for a lifetime of financial and time freedom. They have to build and strengthen their beliefs to take network marketing seriously."

The Company

Most of the women millionaires built belief in their respective companies. They attended meetings, seminars and conventions to gain more information. They decided on the company that best suited their individual needs.

Brenda Loffredo already had a belief in network marketing, but she could not choose a company. "My husband and I tried our hands in a few companies part time trying to decide whether to represent a product or a service," she remembers. "It took us a few companies for us to find one we were best geared towards and that was best geared towards us...In my network marketing company, there is no ceiling. You can make as much as I do, or I can make as much as you do without restrictions on pay structure or gender. It's truly unlimited potential." Now, Brenda enjoys the lavish benefits of that company and plans to pass down her business to her son.

Marilyn Stewart already had a company in mind, but she was hesitant to take a risk. The potential of the company emboldened her. "I didn't know what I was stepping into," she recalls. "I just knew what I wanted to achieve, and I found a company that gave me the freedom to achieve it. I was just an ordinary person willing to do what it takes. What I love about this industry and my company is you get to choose how you want to do this business. It's wide open."

The Products or Services

Most of the women millionaires used the products before they ever considered entering the business. The products improved their lives, so they naturally felt inclined to share the products with friends and family members. For several of these women, their business began to grow before they even knew what they were doing. They truly and passionately believed in their products.

When Rachele Nichols needed extra cash after her family took a financial blow on 9/11, she thought about the products. "I started by using the products of the company. I loved these products, and I knew I needed to get into some kind of retail to pay off our student loans." Her unfaltering belief in the products pointed her in the right direction. Rachele is now a top earner at her company.

For Marcella Vonn Harting, the products meant life or death. Her daughter, as an infant, had actually died in her husband's arms. Although the physicians managed to revive her, Marcella felt determined to provide her daughter with the best health care options available. "My daughter's brush with death changed my life. That directed my life into health, nutrition and wellness. I was literally looking for everything that could make a difference for her. That's how I came into the network marketing industry – searching for great products. Network marketing has great companies with exceptional products. What a difference those products made in our lives." The nutritional products helped her daughter, her family and Marcella reach her dreams.

Cook Up the Big Picture

I confess that I did not understand the difference between visions and goals for a long time. One day, while flipping through the channels on television, I saw a "Wedding Show" that changed my entire perspective. The bride entered a pastry shop and asked, "Will you suggest a wedding cake for me?"

The chef was not helpful, so the woman left the store in frustration. When she entered the next pastry shop and asked the same question, the chef enthusiastically responded, "Sure! Step into our showroom, and I'll show you what might be perfect for your wedding." The room had five fully decorated models of cakes. The chef gave the bride samples to taste. She made her choice within minutes.

This show helped me understand the importance of the big picture. The chef in the first store did not help the bride see how the cake would look. Without a clear picture, she could not make a decision. As the saying goes, "A confused mind does nothing." The second chef,

---

A Success Bite

Vision is the Model of the Big Picture.

Goals are the Action Steps you take to Build the Model.

---

however, did present the bride with options. She could see, taste and smell the various cakes.

With a clear vision, the bride could take action. The same is true in network marketing — the vision is the model, or the big picture of the end result. Goals are the action steps you take to build the model.

Not everyone understands the big picture immediately. Kathy Aaron, who is now an influential businesswoman, admits that she struggled at the beginning. "I have to be honest. I didn't understand the concept of network marketing — a lot of people doing a little bit, being a part of something bigger than themselves. I needed to see the big picture. I went to an event, and I saw 10,000 excited and motivated people. I saw a bigger picture of this industry. The minute I 'got it,' I resigned from my real estate career and went cold turkey into network marketing for the residual income." Now, she enjoys the freedom to control her own time and the financial benefits of her company.

A Success Bite

"Believe in the Unseen" "Believe It, to See It"
When building a successful home-based business,
first you must believe in the unseen. Build belief with
facts about the industry, company and products!

---

8 – Third Ingredient: Take Action

Are You Ready?

Imagine sitting in a fancy restaurant. A woman walks in, sits down and asks the waitress, "Can you just bring me what you think I'd like for dinner?" In this scenario, the waitress would probably reply, "I'll come back when you are ready." Before taking action, you need to make a decision--be ready.

A Success Bite

"Once you make a decision, the universe conspires to make it happen."
- Ralph Waldo Emerson

Energy Vibrations

Have you ever been thinking about a loved one when they called at that exact moment? Surprised, you exclaim, "I was just thinking about you!" Is this magic? Scientific law? Coincidence?

Scientific Law

Everything on the planet, even our thoughts, is a form of energy. Energy creates vibrations, which are sent out into the universe like radio waves. The vibrations cannot be seen by the naked eye, but they are incredibly influential. People respond not only to the words you say, but also to your energy vibrations. You can sway other people's behavior with your energy patterns. You are either sending out a high-attractor energy pattern or a low-attractor energy pattern.

With regards to energy, like attracts like. In other words, similar thought vibrations attract one another. In the phone call example, you were thinking about your friend at the same time as they were thinking about you. Even though you may be in completely different parts of the world, your thought vibrations attracted each other. Distance does not matter.

High-Attractor Energy Patterns

Renowned scientist, Dr. David Hawkins, outlined his research on energy patterns in his book, <u>Power vs. Force: The Hidden Determinants of Human Behavior</u>. According to the book, the central nervous system has the capacity to differentiate between life-supportive and life-destructive patterns.

Hawkins discovered that when a person is placed in a life-supportive pattern (or high-attractor energy pattern), the brain releases endorphins. These chemicals have a pleasing effect on all of the body's organs. In addition, Hawkins noted that attractor patterns tend to dominate any field. Therefore, you can instantly change your mood by placing yourself in a more positive energy field.

Low-Attractor Energy Patterns

Hawkins' book also describes the effects of being in a life-destructive energy pattern. The body responds in a variety of ways- adrenaline is released, the heart rate increases, and the immune system is suppressed. All bodily functions are focused on warding off the negative stimulus, real or imagined.

Energy in the Marketplace

Energy not only influences individual reactions but the outcome of a business endeavor as well. "Attractor fields can be quickly calibrated, whether in product, company or employee," writes Hawkins. "In our research, the differences between business that have failed and businesses that have succeeded have proved so marked that excellent predictive accuracy can be expected."

According to Hawkins, companies that promote human value and service to others in a warm and energetic environment have high-attractor energy fields. These organizations are far more successful than businesses that do not create this atmosphere. "Feelings determine purchases," Hawkins reiterates.

A Success Bite

Create a successful home-based business by Taking Actions that promote human value and service to others.

To achieve maximum success in network marketing, take action with a high-attractor energy pattern. Clear thoughts and beneficial beliefs will help you find the resources needed to reach your goals. However, you cannot reach your goals without taking action that supports human values.

Focused Intention

Intention is like the yeast in a loaf of bread. Both are catalysts that bring the process into fruition. When you act with intention, you have a specific purpose or goal.

An Exercise in Focusing Intention

Imagine a collection of ingredients on the top of your kitchen counter: flour, sugar, eggs, baking cocoa, milk, oil, chocolate chips and vanilla. Your mental task is to mix these ingredients together and bake a delicious chocolate cake. Close your eyes. Go!

What happened? Were you confused? Did you know what proportions of each ingredient were needed without a recipe? In the end, did you give up out of sheer frustration?

This is the way most people start in network marketing. Their minds are scattered, they fumble around and they give up out of frustration. This does not need to happen.

Try one more time. This time, however, here is a recipe to follow:

1 coffee mug
4 tablespoons of flour
4 tablespoons of sugar
2 tablespoons of baking cocoa
1 egg
3 tablespoons of milk

157

3 tablespoons of oil
3 tablespoons of chocolate chips
A splash of vanilla

Add dry ingredients to the coffee mug and mix well.
Add the egg and mix thoroughly. Pour in the milk and
oil, and mix well. Add the chocolate chips (optional)
and vanilla. Mix again.

Put the mug into the microwave and cook for three
minutes at 1000 watts. The cake will rise over the top
of the mug, but don't be alarmed! Allow the cake to
cool and tip out onto a plate. You are ready to eat!

What happened this time? You were probably less confused. Perhaps you could even make this delectable treat right now. The recipe provided a step-by-step plan of how to get the end result. In network marketing, you need both positive intention and a plan to move to action.

```
┌─────────────────────────┐
│                         │
│   A Success Bite        │
│                         │
│   Focus attention on    │
│  building and maintaining│
│  life-long relationships.│
│                         │
└─────────────────────────┘
```

The Intention to Build Relationships

The bottom line of network marketing is building and keeping relationships. How did the women millionaires turn their ability to build relationships into an empire? They focused their intention on building and maintaining life-long relationships.

The women millionaires set out to build relationships with intention. Many discovered that they had the natural ability to do so. "I am a passionate person," says Holly Warnol. "I like helping people. Now I'm making a difference with what I love to do." Because she intended to establish quality relationships with people, Holly effectively created an empire of supportive, caring volunteers.

Model Yourself After Successful People

Conscientiously choose to model yourself after people who have sustainable success. Mirror both their actions and their high-attraction energy patters. As one powerful woman, Sandi Cohen, says, "If there are others who have done it before, there is no reason why you can't also. Know and believe that this industry creates more millionaires than any other. Never give up. Focus your intentions." With a role models as a guide, you can do anything.

The Numbers Game Versus the Quality Game

The Women Millionaire's Club seems to be divided into two camps: those who play the numbers game and those who play the quality game. One approach is not necessarily better than the other. Choose one, and commit yourself to action.

Those who play the number game focus on building as many relationships as possible. They believe that success is based on the number of people you interact with.

Julie Newcomb understands the numbers game: "In this industry, 95% come into the business as wholesale buyers and hobbyists. Only 3-5% comes into the business to build a business. We need everybody. Appreciate everybody at whatever level they want to participate."

The quality game, on the other hand, emphasizes high-caliber relationships. Those who play this game target specific prospects whom they believe will be successful. In this game, your individual success is based on the success of others.

Carole Escolano is a proponent of the quality approach. "I knew I didn't have time, as a mom, to make it about numbers," she says. "So I choose to nurture quality relationships with quality people who were self-starters. I targeted people that were already successful in their careers. I attracted few numbers but a high caliber of people."

Again, one approach has not proven to be better than the other. Pick a strategy based on your own skills and commitment. Then, dive in and get started!

Keep it Simple
In its simplest form, network marketing is a relationship business. If you focus only on that aspect of the business, you will do well. Dianne Leavitt understands this: "I really cling to simple things. It's in my personal character. I think others do too. Network marketing is all about building long-term relationships."

With a simple goal in mind, the work seems less daunting, especially if you enjoy being around people. There is no complex secret to network marketing. Donna Johnson, a network marketing superstar, can attest to this: "This business is so simple. I always keep it about people - meeting people, caring about people, and genuinely seeing those people as people."

Encourage People

```
┌─────────────────────────┐
│                         │
│    A Success Bite       │
│                         │
│   Catch People Doing it │
│   Right! Encourage Others! │
│                         │
└─────────────────────────┘
```

In network marketing, your most important asset is your network of people. Since this network is a volunteer army, you must learn people skills. Most importantly, if you catch someone doing something right, encourage them. Build up the person's confidence. You can create a team of strong, self-sufficient leaders.

Kathy Aaron understands the importance of supporting her team. "I surround myself with a group of leaders that are as successful or more successful than I am," she says. "I don't think I refer to my organization as 'my organization' but more as 'our team.' Leverage the wisdom and knowledge of the leaders. Let people know they are a part of the team. Catch them doing it right." Only with praise and constant encouragement can people feel determined to succeed.

Money comes when you feel passionate about helping others. Jodi Whittemore says, "Really invest in other people. Make people feel important. It is good to be encouraging. Relationship building is core." When you help other people feel strong, your entire team will grow. People cling to enthusiasm and positivity.

The key to helping others is to listen. Eileen Cohen suggests, "Find out what they are interested in and what their needs are so you can help them improve their life." When you listen to people, you can gain a better understanding of their hopes and fears. Only then can you really help someone. As Julie Newcomb says, "Hear what their dreams are. How can you serve them and advocate for them if you don't know them?" Listen and pay close attention to the person's moods. Learn how to improve their lives by catering to their individual needs.

Be Coachable and Find a Mentor

When you first get started in network marketing, put your ego aside. Let those people who have already paved the path show you the way. Allow others to assist you in starting the business properly. If you do not have a mentor, actively seek one out. Find someone who will share their philosophy and strategies with you. A mentor's guidance can really accelerate your business. Nearly all of the women millionaires selected mentors within their businesses. Those who did not have a mentor within their company still sought them out in books. These women did not wait; instead, they actively searched for an admirable person to guide them.

Do not be afraid to learn. One amazing woman, Joyce Dell, warns that you will crash and burn without a mentor. She says, "Be coachable. The kiss of death is to do it your own way when you are starting with a company. Do not reinvent the wheel. Follow the company's system. Make the first million our way. Then, the next million can be done your way. Usually, the proven system seems to work." There is a reason why the company has created a business plan for others to use. These plans were shown to work, so be prepared to learn the system that is already in place.

Be somewhat picky about the person you choose to be your mentor. As Sandi Cohen knows, a mentor can make or break your career in network marketing. "One of my mentors is the author Jim Rohn. He's my mentor, as I read everything he writes and listen to his tapes. He has been around forever. The man is a genius," she says. You are only as successful as those who teach you.

Be Authentic, Loyal, and Passionate

In all of my interviews, each woman repeatedly showed great passion for their work. They each have a genuine enthusiasm for their products, services and companies. Just ask businesswoman Sherrie Olp. "Love what you are doing," she maintains. "Make sure you are hooked up with a company you love and a product you love. Be authentic about how you share your products with others. There is a huge difference between selling and being truly authentic about what you have." Consumers can recognize and embrace a seller who is truly dedicated to the product and the company.

Give Inoculations

Most mothers give their children inoculations to immunize the child against infection and minimize the severity of any future infections. In network marketing, new distributors need inoculations against psychological "infections." They are often plagued by self-doubt and fear of failure. Women millionaires help new distributors toughen up by supporting the belief that 'There is no failure, only feedback.' Each challenge is a form of feedback to teach a new skill or increase belief.

> ## A Success Bite
>
> Inoculate new distributors
> with the belief ...
> "There is no such thing as
> failure, only feedback."

Jodi Whittemore says, "I'd like to inoculate consultants from taking rejection personally, to not be attached to the outcome. I have learned that most of what we worry about never happens. We make up stories in our own minds of what people are thinking, and they are probably not even true. So, if you are going to make up stories, make up positive ones that emphasize that you really care and are listening, that you have their best interest at heart. I want to have them inoculated from the infection of negative people that will try to steal their dreams." With Jodi's encouragement, many new consultants have learned to overcome their fears and to reach their highest potentials.

Persevere through Obstacles

Women millionaires are not held back by obstacles. Instead, they see them as gifts, as opportunities for improvement. Each obstacle helps these women grow stronger and more determined. Marilyn Stewart knows the value of a challenge: "I see obstacles as gifts. They put me in a position to see what I could do, and I look for a solution to solve each challenge." Marilyn's positive attitude helps her overcome any obstacle with a newfound tenacity and strength.

A common and painful obstacle can be repeated no's. Women millionaires are not deterred by negative responses. They stick to their goals and apply consistent effort. Despite facing rejection, Rachele Nichols never gave up. "I didn't let the no's bring me down and make me quit," she says. "For every 100 no's, you get one fabulous consultant. It's a numbers game. Make the numbers work for you." Perseverance is necessary for fulfilling a long-term dream.

Set Goals

Women millionaires take charge and operate their network marketing businesses like CEOs. They have job requirements for each incoming consultant. Most importantly, however, each woman defines her company's success with clear goals. Each woman documents her goals on paper and prepares strategies for reaching these goals.

Carole Escolano was very organized and practical about setting goals. "I started with a goal sheet," she remembers. "I itemized what it was that I had, my strengths, and when I wanted to achieve each goal. Without a time limit, it is just a dream. I put my goals in writing. When people come to me and ask me for my secret for success, I give them a magic bullet – make goals and write them down. And yet, only three out of every 100 will do it." Those three are the consultants most likely to achieve millionaire status.

```
┌─────────────────────────────┐
│                             │
│     A Success Bite          │
│                             │
│        100% of the          │
│   Women Millionaires had    │
│         WRITTEN             │
│    Goals and Visions!       │
│                             │
└─────────────────────────────┘
```

Kathy Aaron also recognizes the benefits of goal setting. "Write your vision and your goals down," she advises. "My mentor helped me create the vision and goals for my business. I have had this vision for 17 years. I had everything written down and mapped out. If someone had woke me up in the middle of the night and asked about my business, I could have told them exactly what my business would look like and how I was going to get there."

Take Action

Network marketing requires committed action. When your team performs the necessary actions, your business will take off. Susan Walsh is a professional motivator. She says, "Get your team into action. Where there is no action, there is no friction. Where there is no friction, there are no results. We get our team into massive action."

Most people get into a home-based business with the belief that they will 'try to' succeed or 'do their best' to succeed. The women millionaires didn't 'try to' succeed instead they 'decided' to succeed. They dedicated themselves to a long-term plan. Even if they did not see immediate results, these women stayed committed for two years, three years, and even longer to turn their dreams into a reality. As Sandi Cohen says, "It is a three to five year commitment to own your own business." With a concerted effort, the women millionaires created and led massive action-oriented teams.

Be Consistent

For people who have been involved in the corporate world, the shift to network marketing can sometimes be overwhelming. With less structure, these people cannot always handle such freedom. Women millionaires learned to structure their daily activities. They make their businesses a top priority and stay away from distractions.

A Success Bite
Take Consistent Action to learn what you do not know. Take Consistent Action to repeat what you do know until it is perfected.

Julie Newcomb, a shining example of marketing success, reinforces consistency. "Knowing, believing and understanding that with a home-based business, you don't have to do it full time, but if you do it consistently and long enough, you can succeed." With consistent effort, you can hone your skills and practice until the process is perfected.

Time management is an essential component of consistency. Many women millionaires practice time-blocking and designate chucks of time to their businesses. Doni Smith understands the benefits of time-blocking. Not only did she set aside time to dedicate to her business, but Doni also organized her time well. She says, "I took slivers of time that I worked with my business. Although learning is extremely important, my revenue-producing time was not the time to be doing my learning or studying." She knew exactly when and for how long to dedicate to each task.

Training

Women millionaires train themselves. They read books and listen to CDs. They do not wait for their sponsor to train them. Any business owner needs to take responsibility and to find help when needed.

Susan Walsh always had an entrepreneurial spirit. When she ran her own hair salon, she learned how to take responsibility. She applied her desire for improvement to her network marketing business. "Create a business that matches your WHY and that includes training, training, training." Susan did not wait around and complain. She took control of her own training and sought helpful information from others.

Prospecting

The network marketing industry was originally called "friendship marketing." Your success depends on your relationships with others. Your most important task is to find like-minded people with whom you can develop a long-term friendship relationship.

Between the number of business and social networking groups on and off the internet, never before have there been so many different ways to interact with people. There are numerous opportunities for you to reach out. Whatever interests you have, there is an online social group of like-minded people who have that same interest. As Dianne Leavitt says, " I have a deep belief in my products and company. I help people with enthusiasm and sincerity and make lots of friends along the way." The beauty of network marketing is that it is based on helping others and achieving success for everyone involved.

The Fortune is in the Follow Up

Most prospects do not join the business right away. They need time to grapple with the decision. Create a follow up system that will allow you to reconnect with your prospects. Women millionaires use everything from a simple notebook to a sophisticated ACT or FileMaker Pro computer program. Use whatever works best for you. The key is to follow up.

Sandi Cohen understands the longer people go without joining the company, the less likely they are to do so. "Understand that you have 90 days to lock people into a business relationship before they disappear," Sandi advises. Even if the follow up fails to produce a business partner, keep the relationship in tact—friendship marketing. You never know who or when they will show up at your door looking for your products or service.

Duplication

The simpler your business is to join, the more attractive the opportunity will be to your prospects. Help people along the way. As Sherrie Olp says, "Show your knowledge. You know more than the person you are teaching. You must be the expert. Show how to duplicate the process." Be a guide and mentor to newcomers. Direct them down the path to success.

Women millionaire Barbara Freundt lays out simple steps for duplication. First, you must understand the business by training yourself. When you contact a prospect, discover their goals. Introduce the business concept. You may need to repeat the concept multiple times before the person fully grasps the idea. Next, outline the various options available in your business. In other words, do they want Retail products? Wholesale? Business Opportunity? The final step, according to Barbara, is to help them understand the products and the selling strategies. Using high-attractor energy patterns emphasizing human value combined with a simple step-by-step duplication process, you are sure to attract a group of enthusiastic consultants.

9 – The Fourth Ingredient: Give Thanks

Gratitude is an attitude that generates positive emotions in others. By acknowledging a benefit that you have received or will receive in the future, you help others feel appreciated. According a 1998 Gallup poll, around 54% of Americans claim to express gratitude to God "all the time." 67% show the same gratitude towards others.

Gratitude Pays Off Personally

Research suggests that gratitude can benefit a person's emotional well-being. Grateful people tend to be happier and more forgiving than their less grateful counterparts.

Appreciation Affects Others

Not only does gratitude improve the quality of your life, but it also pays off financially. In a study by Rind and Bordia, restaurant customers tipped higher when servers wrote a simple "thank you" on their bills. Customers feel a personal connection when the seller expresses gratitude.

In a *Journal of Marketing* article, businessman J.R. Carey described how appreciation could impact sales. Carey conducted a study of jewelry store customers. One group

A Success Bite
Thank your clients with written notes.

received a personal "thank you" phone call, and sales jumped by 70%. A second group of customers received the same call but were also notified of an upcoming sale at the store. Sales only increased by 30% in the second group, probably because customers felt that the caller had ulterior motives. A third control group did not receive any "thank you" call. Sales did not increase in this group. Carey's study demonstrates how a simple act of gratitude can propel a business to the next level.

Be Thankful for Everything

Most people are so busy trying to reach their goals that they forget to give thanks for what they already have. Every now and then, pause and relish in the gifts that you have been given in life. Appreciate what you already have.

My Life Lessons of Appreciation

My mother taught me the value of appreciation. She spent the first 12 years of her life in and out of the hospital undergoing operation after operation. Her parents had seven other children to care for and could only visit her in the hospital once a week. Instead of wasting time wishing for a better life, my mother thanked God for everything she had.

My mother's experiences helped me see the good in every experience. She believed: "Be thankful that you can open your eyes and see the men mowing the lawn, for there are some children that will never see. Be thankful you can hear the birds sing, for there are some children that will never hear. Be thankful that you can feel the pain, for there are some children who do not have the gift of pain and without comparison, they will never know the gift of being pain free." She recognized that moments of joy are only as sweet by comparison to moments of pain.

> ## A Success Bite
>
> "If you learn to appreciate more of what you already have, you'll find yourself having more to appreciate."
> -Author Unknown

If you focus on the problems in your life, they will multiply. Appreciate the good, and your life will be filled with happiness and love.

Women Millionaires Express Gratitude

The women millionaires are thankful for their opportunities and their blessings. They use their gifts to help others. As millionaire Dianne Leavitt says, "I have been blessed so greatly that it seems the only proper thing to do is to give back." They strive to help other women become strong and independent.

Holly Warnol is a mother and a successful businesswoman. She appreciates her opportunities to help other moms: "I'm so grateful to be where I am in my life. I can help other moms stay at home with their kids, too." Only when you are appreciative can you really make a difference in other people's lives.

Appreciate Your Results

Gratitude keeps you centered and focused on the main goal of network marketing: helping others. Women millionaires are spiritually strong, intelligent and empowering. They are so thankful for their success that they constantly give back.

Many women, like Donna Johnson, have started charities. She says, "I'm so grateful for my life and now it's all about giving back. I started a charity. It's about the lives I can change. How can I make a difference? How can I share the gift and possibly change a life?" With exceptional results and an attitude of gratitude, Donna pays it forward to people across the nation.

Leave a Legacy

Women millionaires have the opportunities to help others. They leave legacies that make a difference in the lives of others. These empowered women impact people from every walk of life, from their children to women in developing countries.

Doni Smith wants to inspire everyone, especially her children. "I'd like my legacy to be how many lives I have touched. Basically, it's about empowering my children to be all that I believe God has designed them to be. I come from a long line of strugglers. I am grateful that it has stopped here with me," she says. With her success in network marketing, Doni can provide a better life for her children.

Sherrie Olp also wants to make an impression on her family. "I want my legacy to be that I had the ability to keep our family close together. We fund family events that everyone can come to and not worry about money. The legacy of having all the cousins still being close is beautiful." Sherrie's success brought her family closer together.

Other women millionaires spread their influence to as many people as possible. Marilyn Stewart's passion is to mentor thousands of people. "I want to touch one heart that touches another," she says. "That's my legacy: to create heart-to-heart connections." Her daughter Sarah Stewart also creates heart-to-heart connections, "My passion is showing my generation there is a shift that can happen. There are so many possibilities to look forward instead of looking back in scarcity. We have Possibilities!" This universal impact can lead the world in a positive direction.

"My passion is to leave this world a better place, especially for my grandchildren. If I can touch just one life so that one person feels their greatness, then I'll be grateful. I will have made a contribution by helping to change the world for the better," Says Joyce Dell.

Rachele Nichols sees her success as an opportunity to change lives. She loves network marketing, because she is able to help so many people. "By changing as many other people's lives as we can, we can change our whole world's thinking." Like the other women millionaires, Rachele shows how one woman can make the decision to change the world.

Part II -

Women Millionaire Profiles

Rachele Nichols

Rachele's Background

Rachele Nichols is a strong and successful businesswoman millionaire. Together with her husband and son, they are making their dreams come true.

Rachele Nichols was not born into wealth, nor did she possess an MBA. Yet with no prior business experience, she earned millionaire status through her home-based business. Humbly, she gives the full credit of her success to her maker, her family and her outstanding team of business partners and customers.

As a teen, Rachele had big dreams to marry her high school sweetheart, Jerry, and become a teacher. Her early dreams were quickly realized. Rachele and Jerry married and went off to college together.

She managed to pay for her college tuition and to achieve a Bachelor's degree in Elementary Education. Through her hard work and determination, Rachele also earned a Master's degree. After seven years of teaching, Rachele gave birth to her beloved son, Ethan.

With the addition of a new baby to the family, Rachele and Jerry felt financially strained. Teaching was her passion yet her teacher's salary did not bring in enough money to put Ethan into daycare. She felt immense disappointment. Jerry had just completed graduate school and started working at Merrill Lynch. He worked tirelessly between 60 and 80 hours each week and earned even less than Rachele.

To help her family earn more income while spending time with her precious son, Rachele took on extra side jobs. With Ethan in tow, she babysat, cleaned houses and tutored. Even with such strenuous work, Rachele only earned an additional $300 a month.

Along with Rachele's extra odd jobs and Jerry's position in the financial industry, their hard work and determination began to reduce the massive amount of student loans and credit card debt they had accumulated. A flicker of light appeared at the end of their financial tunnel.

Rachele was not looking for a business, but she was open to new opportunities. A friend introduced her to a pure, safe and beneficial skin care line. She fell in love with the products and introduced her sister, Karla Driskill, to the line. They both saw incredible results. Before they knew what they were doing, they automatically began sharing their new discovery with others. Since they were teachers, they educated anyone who would listen.

Rachele recalls, "I started my home-based business with a company that had great products simply with the hopes of paying off my student loans. My first goal was to earn enough money to pay additional on those loans. I thought that if we could get out from under that burden, what a load that would have been off of our family." Rachele saw her home-based business as the opportunity that could give her family financial security.

At the beginning of her business endeavor, Rachele struggled with the social stigmas of network marketing. She thought, "What are others going to think of me? Why would someone with a Master's degree go into network marketing?" Furthermore, her previous experiences with network marketers had been disconcerting. Rachele recalls, "I knew a few people who had started working for a network marketing company, and they kind of stalked me. They called me saying I had to do business with them. I didn't want people to see me like that –a stalker. I didn't want to be perceived as pushy."

Without any experience in direct sales or the skin care industry, Rachele faced other problems right away. She had attracted numerous buyers but only two business partners and one was her sister, Karla.

Rachele's WHY

Each time Rachele felt discouraged and frustrated, she remembered WHY she was doing this business -- her beautiful family. She'd look at the picture of her son and husband and knew that she could persevere no matter what.

Rachele knew the only way to push past the misperceptions of network marketing and the challenges she faced was to learn more. Her life changed when she attended a company-organized presentation by Jerry Conti. His speech focused on **leading with the business opportunity**. Instead of just sharing information about the products, Rachele learned to incite interest in owning a home-based business. She showed customers how to earn an extra income by referring friends to the business.

Within one year, she and her team of business partners had built "a nation of shoppers" and were earning more than enough to be financially stable.

Rachele's Decision to Succeed

Rachele's success was a direct result of her positive attitude, her strong character and her **DECISION** to succeed.

Her first mark of success was in her **decision to succeed**. She decided to make her home-based business her top priority. She began a consistent campaign to learn more about the industry, her company, her products and herself to bolster her own beliefs. Rachele went into massive action. She started running a business.

Rachele's Strengths

Consistency is Key. Rachele says, "Coming from an education background, I saw kids that were naturally brilliant but that wouldn't put in any effort. Then, there were other kids who were not as smart, but who were very consistent. I was just consistent. I had a **'no matter what' attitude**." Even when she had a particularly difficult day, Rachele kept running a business. On occasion, she might quit for a day, but she always restarted her business the next day.

She never gave up, despite facing difficulties and letdowns. When a person said "no," Rachele initially felt hurt. She quickly learned that direct sales were a numbers game. Her husband's financial business helped her learn that for every 100 NO's, you get one client. When people chose not to join her business, Rachele simply moved on to the next person. Rachele and Jerry even made a game of getting NO's. They placed a chart on the refrigerator and celebrated each NO with a 'fridge' countdown. Turning NO's into fun helped her keep her business a business instead of taking it personally. She managed to stay positive and move on.

Rachele learned to cherish people as they are instead of expecting them to be where she wanted them to be. She states, "**I just loved people, and I still do. I love them where they are. I share with them my products and opportunity because I feel I have real gifts for them.**" By treating her customers and team members as 'special', Rachele built solid relationships and formed a network of caring business partners.

Stay Focused. Rachele **managed her time** appropriately. Although she had a spontaneous temperament, Rachele disciplined herself to **stay focused**. She broke up her time into chucks and made the best possible use of each minute.

Hold Others to their Excellence. To succeed you must build teams of people that are moving in a forward direction. "In my company, we sign an independent consultant application. We have to remember we are independent consultants, not co-dependent consultants. I tend to want more for people than they want for themselves. I've learned to support and help people yet hold them to their excellence." Rachele helps her team move forward by leading them to be accountable to themselves and the team. The secret is to find a balance between being too independent and being too dependent.

Everyone Can Make It. Rachele does not see gender as an important factor in business success. For both men and women, the goal is to share the business and the products. The strategies of success are the same for all people. She says, "**The key ingredients that make someone successful in a home-based business are consistent effort, never giving up, not being affected by "no's," and having a long term vision.** I think those key ingredients are critical for anyone to be successful, whether male or female."

Rachele acknowledges and appreciates the personality differences between the two genders. She says that women tend to be more nurturing and more relational. Since network marketing is a relational business, women may even have a leg up. Rachele often refers to network marketing as a "business for yourself, not by yourself." She sets clear boundaries with other people to establish the ideal business relationships. Anyone can achieve success in network marketing, regardless of gender.

Rachele's Ingredients for Success

Rachele's home-based business has made her a millionaire. Others see her as a role model and mentor who willingly shares her time, energy and ingredients for success.

Her **long-term vision is** to help people understand success might not be immediate, but they can reach their goals by continually moving forward.

Rachele propounds a simple system of success:

1. Accountability
Rachele takes personal accountability seriously and helps others do the same. She is an active member of several accountability groups that she facilitates or is part of on a weekly basis. Accountability group members share their goals, share their progress, share their successes and share their plans to overcome obstacles.

2. Prospecting
Rachele uses her already established relationships and continually seeks ways to form new ones. Rachele has achieved her incredible success by using and expanding her social network.

3. Presenting
Rachele shares her presentation with as many people as possible, as often as possible. The more she tells the story of

her company and products, the more relationships she creates.

4. Following Up
According to Rachele's philosophy, "the fortune is in the follow up." Many people who originally turned her down later changed their minds. She keeps in touch and follows up with all customers.

5. Training
Rachele believes training is key to building a successful home-based business. She trains others and goes to ongoing training on the products, the company, and the industry.

Rachele's Legacy

Rachele's passion is to assist others in reaching their full potentials and discover the greatness that lies within. She experienced tremendous **personal growth** through her home-based business and wants the same for others. She says, "My obligation to myself is to become as great as I can possibly be and to teach others to see the greatness in themselves."

"I love the way that I can increase my income by helping other people increase their incomes. We can help so many people achieve excellence with this business. Our company is a vehicle for people to become everything they were ever meant to be."

Rachele's legacy is helping others find their greatness. She believes that by changing as many other lives as possible, she can change the world.

Donna Johnson

Donna's Background

Donna Johnson is a multi-millionaire girl next door. She was raised in a blue-collar family in Wisconsin. Donna's father left when she was 13 years old, and her mother was unable to care for the family. With four brothers, Donna was forced to grow up quickly and started searching for ways to feed the family.

By the age of 19, Donna realized that she did not have the financial resources to attend college. Still, she loved to swim and became a coach. Even with her passion for sports, Donna was still struggling to make money. She searched for ways to supplement her income.

Donna hoped that by marrying the man she loved, she would feel more protected and financial secure. After giving birth to three beautiful children, Donna faced another challenge. The marriage did not provide the protection or financial security she had longed for. Sadly, the marriage ended and Donna became the sole provider for her small children at the age of 29.

With no college degree, no financial stability and nowhere to turn, many people would have felt trapped. Instead of crying or making excuses, Donna set goals and looked for ways to improve her situation. As fate would have it, Thea O'Donoghue introduced her to a home-based business.

Donna Decided to Succeed

Donna was intrigued with the thought of owning her own business. A success pattern that clearly runs throughout her life is her DECISION to succeed.

Donna **DECIDED** to own a home-based business. The moment she committed, she knew she would make it a **successful** home-based business. "I knew what I needed to do. It wasn't a 'get rich quick' scheme. I knew I couldn't do it for a season and then become a millionaire. I rolled up my sleeves and did what it took to be successful." She felt especially encouraged after seeing an infomercial with Rita Davenport. The two women met at a national conference and bonded immediately. With Rita as her mentor, Donna felt motivated to succeed.

Donna's WHY

Donna's success, however, did not come quickly. She struggled to **re-engage every day.** Donna recognized the constant work involved in owning a home-based business and decided to stick with it no matter what. Her WHY carried her through the tough times. She wanted her children to see their mom as a strong and independent woman who did not need to lean on anyone. They'd know that mom worked hard, yet she worked from home to schedule her life around family. Her WHY kept her focused.

The Benefits of Being a Woman

Donna believes that women and men face different challenges. Women already have a motherly instinct that is extremely beneficial in network marketing. On the other hand, Donna claims that women face the challenge of being a Mother Theresa figure and trying to "drag people across the finish line." Women need to let go of that urge to be overly helpful.

According to Donna, network marketing provides a unique opportunity for women. Anyone can be successful, even with very little money. She says, **"Use the positive parts, the virtuous parts, of being a woman to build a business."** The industry allows women to develop their **intuitions** and leadership skills. **Donna associates building a business with building a family - the leader is a person who others can trust.**

The Benefits of Network Marketing

Network marketing is an **even playing field**. The company's compensation plan is the same for both genders and for people with varying levels of education. However, one benefit for women is the personal connections that are needed. Donna says that when women meet new people, they **"genuinely care and see those people as people, not dollar signs."** This ability to relate to others is a real asset for women in network marketing.

188

Network marketing is an ever-changing industry. Donna appreciates this aspect: "**I am constantly learning and growing. I think that it is vital to stay current**. You either stay green and are watered, or you die on the vine." A common myth is that when you reach a certain big bucks position in any company you can take vacations and stop working. However, network-marketing companies are not structured this way. It takes consistent forward movement.

Donna's Ingredients for Success

1. Manage Your Expectations.
When new consultants ask Donna for help, she first advises them to manage their expectations. Donna often meets people who expect to make millions within the first 10 minutes of business. She says, "**They are not patient. They are used to trading hours for dollars, and when success doesn't come instantly, they move on. They are distracted.**" This is the most common mistake. A home-based business is just like building a house-it takes a while to build a strong foundation. Be patient. Financial rewards only come once your foundation is built.

2. Appreciate the Lifestyle.
A home-based business is not just about the financial rewards, it's also about appreciating the benefits of the lifestyle. Consultants achieve personal growth, establish new relationships and have the freedom of running a business

from home. These are benefits that cannot be found in other jobs.

3. Focus on Long Term Goals.
Donna advises others to focus on **long term goals** instead of immediate results. Start with the end in mind and build toward that. Donna started with the picture of a successful business and wrote goals to achieve that picture.

4. Be Coachable.
The people who are open to coaching by those who have already succeeded attain success faster than those that reinvent the wheel. By helping others find financial peace, Donna is giving back to her community. She personalizes each new business partner's business plan to help them achieve what they need and want.

5. Use a System.
Donna truly believes that almost anyone who is coachable and can follow the simple steps to building a home-based business can be outrageously successful. Donna declares, "**I challenge anyone. If you can manage your expectations, can be coachable and actively follow the system, then you can do this job.**"

6. Stay Active.
As with any **entrepreneurial business**, Donna learned to stay active. She says, "You cannot become complacent in this business, but isn't that the same with life as well? Do you want to become complacent in your life? It's not just this

190

industry. **I continually do appointments, share this product, show this business and build a team."** With constant activity, anyone can succeed.

Consultants need to keep working each day to reach their goals. Donna loves the active lifestyle: **"I am passionate about the business, and I love what I do.** I just took my twins to school. What am I going to do now? Sit and watch soap operas all day? I don't think so. My life challenges have kept me actively moving toward new goals."

7. Help Others

Instead of resting on her eminent success, Donna consistently helps others. This business is about helping others succeed. When they succeed she believes it helps her evolve as a businesswoman.

Donna understands the importance of helping others: **"God gave us the tools to do this, to take the gifts that we've been given and to utilize them. He wanted us to live in contribution, not in entitlement."** Through her constant effort, Donna exhibits this quality every day.

8. Have Fun

Most importantly, Donna has fun with her business. She enjoys meeting people and helping them discover their business' potential. Donna says, "If you love what you do, it's not work. It's fun." This kind of attitude brought Donna incredible success.

Donna's Legacy

Donna's motto "Soar on your Spirit Wings" was taken from an old Joni Erickson song that she felt was inspirational. Joni was a bright and beautiful teenage girl when she had a swimming accident and became a paraplegic. Still, Joni persisted and met her challenges head on. She learned to paint with a brush in her mouth. She became an outstanding singer.

One song, called "Spirit Wings," particularly touched Donna. She recalls a line that says, "You lift me above all the earthly things." This line encouraged Donna to push herself and to reach her goals. She says, "I always carried that vision with me. I loved the idea that I could be lifted up above any circumstance to better myself, to improve myself, and to change my life." Joni's lyrics are appropriate, given Donna's challenging upbringing. Donna is a role model and mentor for all people who have hopes of a better brighter future. Her legacy is to Make a Difference.

Network marketing is about giving. Since she has been blessed to grow and achieve success, Donna founded a charity called "Spirit Wings Kids." The charity funds children in crisis situations and provides assistance families. It is Donna's greatest joy to be able to change lives: **"It is so inspiring to me to be in a business where I always have the opportunity to make a difference."**

Eileen Cohen

Eileen's Background

Eileen Cohen is a posh millionaire. She has to pinch herself daily. She feels so blessed to be living her dream lifestyle, where if she wants something she goes out and buys it. In fact, she attended an auto show and purchased a loaded Lexus IX 350 the day after the show. With this **millionaire mindset**, Eileen can lead a lavish lifestyle. She wakes without an alarm clock, takes cruises through South America, and her paycheck still increases. Her home-based business afforded her this dream lifestyle.

Eileen's life was not always so extravagant. Although she always had an **entrepreneurial spirit**, Eileen's background is in real estate. Along with her husband, she built homes and invested. They had a comfortable lifestyle. Then, the real estate market crashed and Eileen's family lost everything. The family was forced to move into one of their rental homes.

It was time for a make a major change. The couple decided to enter into the satellite and cable industry. They had to pay a high price: uprooting their family and moving to San Antonio. Eileen reflects on that difficult time: "I had two children in high school and one in elementary school. The worst thing you can to is to pull your kids out of high school, especially between semesters. I couldn't even let them finish the year." She felt guilt and the pressure to shoulder much of the responsibility.

Life in San Antonio was not easy. Eileen was forced to return to the real estate industry. The lifestyle was strenuous. Eileen worked nights and weekends to support the family. Vacations were never an option. Eileen and her family returned to California for two years and then moved to Arizona.

Eileen Decided to Succeed

Eileen wanted a business with residual income. She answered an ad that introduced her to a network marketing company; she **decided** to take the risk. Her husband was not happy. Convinced network marketing was a scam, he was unsupportive. He requested that she refrain from selling to friends and family.

Distraught, Eileen said, "I basically started my business with my hands tied behind my back. Yet, I decided I would succeed." Eileen began her business under difficult circumstances. With a will of steel, she **Decided to Succeed**. She would not let anyone or anything stop her from becoming a success.

Eileen's WHY

Eileen longed to have time and financial freedom, which she could only achieve by leaving the real estate business. She says, "I started with a **vision** that I wanted out of real estate. **I wanted my own life. My 'why' was so great. I think this is the key. You have to know why you are doing the**

business." Determined to succeed, Eileen continued to work part time in real estate for a year. At the same time, she diligently worked her home-based business.

Eileen understood the long-term **dedication and focus** that was needed to succeed in network marketing. Although her first few paychecks were small, Eileen held her ground and built a solid foundation for her business. She recalls, "For me, the business was going to give me freedom – freedom from being at everyone's beck and call, freedom not to worry about money, and freedom to be there to help my children." After years of effort, Eileen finally achieved the freedom that she desired.

Eileen knew network marketing worked. She struggled through seven companies trying to find the right company, the right leadership, the right products and the right people with whom to build her business. Along the way, she connected with Sandi Cohen, who was searching for a way out of financial nightmare. Eileen encouraged Sandi to discover the power of residual income through network marketing. At first Sandi was not interested.

Through Eileen's persistence, the two became dear friends. Eileen's tutelage helped Sandi become enamored with owning a home-based business. Sandi later returned the favor by introducing Eileen to the company where her skills and knowledge were perfectly matched for success. The two forged lifelong bonds of friendship. Both are members of the Women's Millionaire Club.

Eileen's Strengths

By visualizing her success, Eileen was able to focus on making that dream into a reality. She says, "I had my mind set that I was going to be successful. I saw myself having that lifestyle, and I was **determined to be successful.** There was not a doubt in my mind. **I saw the vision.** I saw the opportunity to make a difference." Financial success is not possible without hope.

For Eileen, failure was not an option. She stayed strong. Eileen recalls, "As with any business, there are nay-sayers out there. Whenever I ran into a negative person, **I put up a barrier and a shield, so I didn't hear negative talk. The negativity didn't affect me. The bullets could fly, but unless I let them penetrate me, they wouldn't. I didn't have time to be pulled down.**" By staying positive, Eileen made her business dreams come true.

Another benefit for Eileen was finding a great company with excellent products. She could easily follow the compensation plan. The company also provided a solid and simple strategy for success. Eileen could genuinely support and sell the products.

The Benefits of Being a Woman

According to Eileen, men and women are both suited for network marketing. Women bring the strengths of building relationships and helping others. "Men bring the strength of numbers and bottom line strategies. By combining both of these skills, men and women can build strong, successful businesses.

Eileen's Ingredients for Success

Eileen offers three ingredients for success to develop long-lasting relationships.

1. Discover The Interest.
First, **find out what people are interested in**. If possible, begin with your warm markets, which are already based on **trust**. For various reasons, some business partners may not be able to use their warm markets. Eileen was not permitted to sell her products to friends and family. Other consultants may find that friends and family are not interested. In this case, **discover what makes people comfortable and begin a relationship there.**

2. Discover the Need and Want - and Listen.
Eileen's second ingredient is to **find out what people need and want**. Some people only want to buy products. Some people want to earn a few extra dollars by working part time. Others want to become full time business builders. According to Eileen, listening is the best way to help others improve their lives.

3. Ask Questions
The last ingredient is to **ask questions**. When consultants ask questions, they can relate to their customers better. They

can determine more easily how interested the customers are in the business. Pay attention to how excited people are about the products and the business opportunity.

Eileen's Legacy

Eileen hopes her legacy is that she has Made a Difference in the lives of others.

With over 16,000 people in her organization, Eileen has impacted the lives of many people. She has helped so many people change their health, their financial situations and their lifestyles. The one thought that keeps her motivated: "Had I not gotten started in this business, all of these people's lives would not have been touched by this product and their lives would not have been changed. That's huge to me."

That desire to help others is what makes Eileen such a strong, influential woman. Her legacy is the impact she continues to make on others.

Julie Newcomb

Julie's Background

Julie Newcomb, a bright and hardworking woman, always knew that she had the ability to lead. As a child, Julie gathered all of the neighborhood children together to play kick the can. When summertime came around, she felt determined to start a club. She fondly recalls, "I would start a club and get all these people to join, but I was so bossy that they'd quit. Ha! Lesson number one learned. So, I'd have to recruit more kids." In high school, she was a cheerleader. With her outgoing, tenacious personality, Julie has always been well suited to be an entrepreneur.

When Julie became an adult, real world problems hit her hard. Her world collapsed when her husband plunged the family into bankruptcy. She lost everything– her car, her home, her financial security and her marriage. The bankruptcy was a 10-year albatross hung around her neck. Her three children looked to her for leadership. She had a son entering college, a daughter in high school and a young daughter in a private Christian school. In spite of the fact that she had a teaching degree, she was always able to stay at home and raise her children. At age 42, the weight of the world was placed upon squarely Julie's shoulders. Julie had to start over.

Her father was an important figure in Julie's life. He instilled an **entrepreneurial spirit** in her. However, after the bankruptcy, Julie found herself in a deep financial and emotional pit. She hoped that she could ask her father for a position in his company. She says, "That would have been wonderful. He would have sent me home at 3:30 or 4:00 to take care of the kids. I would have had benefits."

But her father had recently passed away. She sank even further into depression. Options were running out. In deep financial debt, Julie feared for her future. She wondered where she would be ten years down the road. She feared that at any point, an entry-level college student could take her position in a company.

Julie Decided To Succeed

Regardless of her difficult situation, Julie refused to give up. She **decided** to make a change so she could succeed. She wanted to create the right work opportunity where she could thrive instead of just survive: **"I had to have security with no ceiling on my income. Most of all, whatever I did had to be fun. I may not have had any money, but fun was my number one priority. I wanted time freedom to be with my family."** She despised jobs in which she was told what to do and when to do her work. "Take oxygen away but don't make me work for someone else!" said Julie. Freedom was essential for her.

At that point, a woman named Rita Davenport changed Julie's life. Rita had a television show called "Open House" in Phoenix, Arizona. When the two women met, Rita told Julie to expect a phone call in regards to a home-based business opportunity. Julie still remembers the day that she received the call: "I was in bed at 3:00 in the afternoon. I was in a deep depression. I had chronic fatigue syndrome from all the stress. And Rita said, 'You have to be at my house at 6:00 pm.' There wasn't much of a warning, and I was a complete wreck." Still, Julie decided to stand up and make a change. **She decided she must succeed no matter what.**

Julie's WHY

Julie's WHY got her out of bed and to her first meeting at Rita's house. Julie's dad always told her, "It's better to be healthy and rich instead of sick and poor." She was so unhappy that she needed a transformation: "I wanted to spend one evening with positive people. So, I went." At Rita's house, Julie met many inspiring women. They spoke of earning trips and having fun with their work. Some had only been in the company for six months. Julie was interested immediately.

The next day, Julie was so intrigued that she attended a second meeting. She saw the benefit of **building relationships** with these women.

At the meeting, the women divided into groups: one that discussed the product and one that discussed the business opportunity. Julie was in the latter group. When she learned about the multiplying circles of business partners and the endless possibilities, Julie thought, "What a brilliant

201

marketing model. I'll get paid for talking and teaching others to talk. Wow...this Network Marketing is made for me." Julie maintains, "People who are successful in Network Marketing are people who like people and people who like helping people."

Julie's father's words, "it is a liability to work for someone else," rang in her ears. She took that as a sign. She finally had hope and immediately signed up. She was now the owner of her own home-based business.

Julie was even more thrilled to learn that the products were high-quality cosmetics, formulated in Switzerland, a Mecca for Skin Care and Nutrition research. She saw firsthand how these cosmetics helped women feel more confident. Julie knew this industry was inflation proof: "Even in hard times, women still wear cosmetics!" The following day, Julie made her first sale to a friend who immediately saw results.

As Julie's business grew, she finally started to feel healthy and more comfortable. "I remember when my check was $3,000 a month. I started sleeping at night. I started breathing. I realized that this company was the real deal," Julie recalls. She felt confident in the products and in the business. She eventually amassed a community of business partner volunteers.

Over the years, she has earned millions through her network marketing business and has the great joy of working closely with her daughter, Jodi Whittemore, who is also in the same home-based business and a member of the Women's Millionaire Club.

Julie's Strengths

Julie was lucky to have a supportive network of friends and family from the beginning. She recognizes that not everyone is as fortunate: "**If someone in your circle of influences is a negative dream stealer, just remember that you and God are a majority. He will give you the vehicle to get you there.**" Despite her illness and financial problems, Julie's strong faith in God helped her stayed positive.

According to Julie, her most important strength is her fear. **Fear motivates** her to get out of bed each morning. Julie remembers, "Every morning, I would pray for 45 minutes in order to get the courage to put one foot on the floor." Fear of failure, fear of not being able to provide for her children, and fear of facing the world motivated Julie to push herself. She learned that fear was "**F**alse **E**vidence **A**ppearing **R**eal!"

Julie consistently used her company's products. The results were immediate. She **felt better and had tons of energy.** Fear motivated her, but her newfound energy propelled her into millionaire status.

She was pleased to find that her company rewarded people for their efforts. This helped Julie gain and develop a strong belief in the company and in the products. Also, the rewards program helped Julie learn to **set written goals**.

Since she always had freedom growing up, Julie never learned to set goals for herself. The company laid out an exact plan of how to reach goals and she unquestioningly followed the plan. She was motivated to get to the fun rewards of exotic trips to faraway places with her entire family. She set her goal to earn every trip the company offered. With each trip she earned, her business grew larger and more income flowed in while she played in the ocean with her kids. Today, she is joined by her young grandchildren on the company trips, along with her children.

Julie gained confidence from helping other women. The business allowed her to help others and to provide a service to women around the nation. Julie describes the feeling of presenting the products to women: **"There was gratitude on their faces for what I was sharing. I noticed that I was beginning to feel valued. I was sharing something valuable with them.** Everyone was having a good time. All of a sudden, I forgot about my challenges. My whole demeanor was about adding value to them. The more I valued them, the more fun I had. Money follows value!" Julie began to love her job and **to have fun** at work.

She took personal responsibility for her own self-development. She went to every program her company offered and became a learning sponge. A favorite saying she picked up at one of the programs is: "Education is never out for the pro. There is always something to learn." Her mentor,

Rita Davenport, taught her, "Put the coins of your purse into your mind and your mind will fill your purse to overflowing!"

Julie's Ingredients for Success

Julie follows a five-step process of recruiting other people. This process, which she learned from Sonya Stringer, is based on influencing others with integrity. The following steps helped Julie achieve enormous success:

1. Relate
In order to recruit people, relate with them. Find something in common and build a relationship on that commonality. Julie says, "They buy you first!"

2. Discover
Eighty-five percent of the conversation should be about discovery. Ask questions about other people. Find out about their lives, their interests and their goals. Listening is the most important aspect of discovery. Listening to the dreams and desires of others can help you learn the best way to serve and support them. She constantly teaches. "People don't care how much you know until they know how much you care," she says.

3. Advocate
Promote the products and the business. Share the opportunities and talk about what the business has to offer them and what involvement with the organization has done for you.

4. Support

Help others become successful. Even if they do not want to join the business, support them in discovering what will make them feel happy and empowered. "Timing is everything. A person might not be interested at first, but things change in six months. Keep in touch," says Julie.

5. Move to Action

Assist others in taking the necessary steps toward success. Constant movement and activity will help you reach your goals.

These ingredients for success may be simple, but putting them into practice can sometimes be difficult. Although Julie wanted to quit on occasion, she persisted. She never considered quitting for more than 24 hours. Instead, she maintained a **"no matter what" attitude** that helped her overcome the difficult moments.

The Benefits of Being a Woman

Julie believes that women have special attributes that help them excel in the business world. Men may be better at training others on the marketing plan or the product; however, as nurturers, women are more caring about their consultants. Women are better at forming trusting and open business relationships.

Still, Julie says that everyone is needed to help the business grow. Gender does not matter, because all companies need a dedicated work force in order to grow. **"We appreciate everybody at whatever level they want to participate. In the industry, 95% of people are wholesale buyers and hobbyists. 3% to 5% are business builders. We need everybody,"** Julie reflects. Each person has a role within the company, regardless of his or her gender or personality traits.

Julie's Legacy

Because of her dedication and effort, Julie is an inspirational figure to women. She hopes that she will be remembered for encouraging others to reach their goals. **"There are so many people that you don't even know today that will be changed just because you did not give up on your dreams,"** Julie says.

Julie feels blessed by the gift of network marketing and spends her time "paying it forward." She says, "How can you have something that you consider such a gift and not want to pay it forward? You must pay it forward to make a difference in this world."

The results of Julie's efforts are amazing, because she devotes herself to loving and caring for other people. She encourages people to attend meetings and to meet new friends. Enthusiasm is critical in network marketing. "It's not what you say, it's how you FEEL about what you say!" says Julie. Other people have so many lessons to learn from Julie's wise teachings and from her incredible story.

Julie's legacy is to inspire other to reach for their dreams. Julie reflects, "It has been said that to love a person is to learn the song that is in their heart and to sing it to them when they have forgotten. You must have faith that there is light at the end of the tunnel. Believe that you may be that light for someone else. Don't be afraid to shoot for the stars. It's great up here and there is room for you, too. See you at the top!"

Carole Escalano

Carole's Background

Carole Escalano is a woman with a long history in network marketing. In fact, many of the women in Carole's down line are also millionaires.

Before her current success, Carole lived a life with many challenges. She was born and raised in the Philippines as one of five children. As the middle child, Carole jokes that "If we were to go by the birth order theory that would make me the politician of the family." Her family was poor, especially after her father abandoned them. Still, her mother continued to work hard and provide for her children. Carole watched her mother struggle and saw a woman that did not stop no matter what. This value propelled Carole to do the same.

With her mother's unyielding belief in her, Carole managed to graduate from St. Paul College with top grades. At age 17, Carole migrated to America and became involved with an IBM program. She took computer-programming courses and hoped to attend graduate school eventually.

Love changed Carole's plans. When she got married, Carole gave up her hopes of graduate school and starting having children. One child was born with Bipolar Disorder, which changed Carole's plans once again. She did not want to leave her children with someone else and looked for a job – one in which she did not have to clock in or clock out. Carole wanted to control her own time.

She thought her only option was to become a real estate agent. She quickly discovered that with real estate, she didn't have to punch a clock - instead she was on the clock 24/7.

One day, a friend invited Carole to a lecture by Dr. Andre St. Augustine, a professor of marketing. She sat stupefied as he unfolded a marketing concept – he was explaining the solution she had been praying for. He said, "Network marketing is a concept where you talk to lots of people and share information about your products or services. You then invite those people to join your home-based organization as a consumer or business builder partner. Your income comes from the efforts of many people doing a little bit. You determine the size of your organization and how diligently you wish to work. You own your own business and receive all the tax benefits that go with that. You are not alone in business as the company you join stands behind you. You have the possibility to make whatever income you decide to make. This marketing concept only works if you do."

Carole Decided To Succeed

From then on, Carole says that she had the "bug." She could not contain herself and felt compelled to spread the word. She **DECIDED**, "If I find the right combination of a great product, company and compensation plan, I will make it." She enthusiastically started a career in network marketing. She knew instinctively, "If you get into network marketing thinking you will fail, then you will fail. I got in it knowing success is just around the corner but I have to study to get there. This is my business and I must know how to make it succeed."

Carole's first step was to educate herself. She threw herself into her studies about network marketing. She read every book about every facet of the home-based business industry. She modeled the actions and skills of successful home-based entrepreneurs. She improved her communications skills and learned to read people. She viewed every failure as a step closer to success. She tweaked her personality and became more cordial and charming. Like her mother, Carole did not stop.

Even with this determined attitude, Carole faced many challenges from the beginning. She had four children to raise and no money to invest. Her marriage was starting to fall apart. Carole's husband and other family members called her crazy. At family functions, Carole was told that she would be kicked out for talking about her new business. The constant disputes and negative comments were extremely hard on Carole. Still, Carole refused to play the victim and held her head high.

She worked her day job from 8 a.m. to 5 p.m. She'd come home get everything ready, pack all four kids in the car, and head across town to give a presentation. She knew that the effort she expended on the front end of her business would yield huge results on the back end.

Carole waited patiently for her success to come. She had seen people get into network marketing have one failure and give up. That was not going to happen to her.

Eventually, she became a founding leader in her company. She was one of the first four distributors to reach $500,000 in her organization. When she finally reached her goals, Carole shared her rewards with those same family members who didn't want her to talk about her home-based business.

Carole's Strengths

Carole sees **her sincere love for others** as her most valuable strength. Her desire to serve others makes her successful in network marketing. "I have always been service oriented. To me, that is the key ingredient of a successful business. It is a journey of service. That is what I think is my very strong attribute," she says.

Her service is based on generosity. Carole met one woman who could not afford to join the company. She could not even fix her car. Carole believed in her ability to succeed and lent her the money. This was not a charity act, as Carole expected the woman to return the payment. This was an investment in the woman and her success. When the woman had the opportunity to repay the loan she felt empowered and valued. Carole's generous attitude helped her reach millionaire status.

Carole's dogged determination is also a strength. "When you give me a problem or challenge, I seek a way to solve the problem, and it's only a matter of time before I find the solution. You can always find a solution. A problem without a solution is called ~ impossibility. I have only solvable problems, not impossibilities," said Carole.

Carole's WHY

Whenever Carole experienced a moment of self-doubt, she relied on her WHY to pull her through. From a very young age, Carole believed she was part of God's creation. He had a reason for her existence. She developed a 'Robin Hood' mentality. If she had a whole fish for dinner, she would cut it in half and feed two more people. What kept her moving forward was her belief that she could help turn one life around and impact many others. As a mom, she started with her own kids and worked her way into the world, impacting one life at a time.

Carole's Ingredients for Success

When Carole first started network marketing, she created a **goal sheet.** She listed her strengths, goals, and what she would need to reach those goals. She says, "I **looked at what was supportive and I looked at what was a challenge so that I could deal with it."** This strategy, according to Carole, is the same used by CEOs of large organizations. They think about how to hire the best employees that will meet these challenges.

Carole's strategy was to be CEO of her home-based business and hire the best. She looked to employ distributors who were already successful in their careers.

Carole's commitment to her family was paramount. With four kids, she didn't have the time to play the numbers game. Instead, Carole played the quality game and only targeted quality people. She conducted interviews to evaluate people's potential for success. During these interviews, Carole initiated heart-to-heart conversations. She was open and direct: "I told them that this was my business and that I wanted them to be a part of a successful team. If they wanted to join, we can achieve a lot of success together." This honest approach promoted a mutual understanding between Carole and her prospects. As a result, Carole was able to enroll people who required very little training.

Carole's Legacy

Carole's mission and legacy is to help women to make an extraordinary living while maintaining their values - to empower women around the globe. Many older adults claim that younger generations do not have the same family values as those in the past. Over 2.2 million young people are incarcerated. Carole says that women have the opportunity to affect the future for their children and the world.

Women are the foundation of the family: "We have to find a way for women to fulfill the basic maternal instinct and to be in charge of taking care of the children." Unfortunately, Carole says, too many women are forced to choose between making a living and having time at home to instill decent values into their children. Carole wants all women to be active parents and to have financial stability and freedom. Network marketing was her solution and she wants others to see it is a viable option for them as well.

Sandi Cohen

Sandi's Background

Sandi Cohen is an incredible woman with a reverse success story. She went from riches to rags before finding success in network marketing.

In high school, Sandi met a freshman in college named Ed, who was studying to be a pharmacist. The two quickly fell in love and married. They prospered in traditional business from the beginning. With five pharmacies in Philadelphia, Ed and Sandi became successful.

Sandi discovered that she, too, had entrepreneurial talents. One day a customer entered the pharmacy in need of supplies. The woman related that her usual pharmacy refused to help her with her supplies or paperwork. Sandi was shocked. She picked up the phone and within minutes solved the dilemma. Sandi saw a niche in the marketplace and quickly filled it. She started a business in medical and surgical supplies, specializing in pediatrics. Within three years, the business exploded and became a multi-million dollar corporation.

Sandi and Ed became extremely prosperous and lived a wildly lavish lifestyle. They owned a 10,000 square foot home. They had an English butler and numerous maids. They traveled in style - a Rolls Royce. They were living the good life. Their accountants assured them they were set for life.

Then the industry changed dramatically. Managed care changed. They had almost no cash flow to run their businesses. The stress was too much to handle, so they sold the business to private investors. They still believed they were comfortable and set for life.

Unfortunately, the private investors defaulted. Sandi and Ed were thrown into in an eight-year legal nightmare. In a landmark decision, Sandi and Ed won their case. However, the settlement was so small that only the lawyers were compensated.

Sandi and Ed were dead right but dead broke. With over $100,000 worth of debt, they lost everything: the cars, the house and the extravagant lifestyle were all gone. The tears welled in their eyes as they watched a friend purchase their home.

They were forced to move. They had fond memories of Phoenix, Arizona, where Sandi had once shopped at the Biltmore Shopping Square in her designer duds. This time they were off to Phoenix, Arizona to start over again. Their only consolation was they would be near their youngest son, who was attending college at ASU.

Sadly, they still had not yet reached the bottom of the downward spiral. Sandi's mother was diagnosed with breast cancer and Alzheimer's. Sandi had vowed never to put her mother into a nursing home. So, Sandi took her mother into her home and took care of her. For five years, Sandi's mother was diapered, tube fed, and suctioned. Life was becoming more and more difficult each day.

Prior to leaving for Phoenix, Sandi felt petrified of starting a new life. One of her staff members wrote down a phone number on a crumbled piece of paper and stuffed it in Sandi's hand. She had said, "When you settle in Arizona, give this lady a call. She's neat. You'll like her." Sandi took her advice and called Eileen Cohen (same last name, but no relation).

Eileen would end up changing Sandi's life. The two women had lunch. Sandi shared her story and cried. Eileen listened attentively. However, when she brought up the idea of network marketing, Sandi thought, "Don't even go there." She was convinced that network marketing was a scam.

Sandi's Decision to Succeed

Sandi realized that she was out of options. She couldn't go back to teaching for only $25,000 a year because she needed that much to get through a month in order to get out of debt. She didn't want to work for a boss. And the thought of owning another pharmacy -with the overhead, equipment, receivables, insurance, and huge investments with even bigger risks - made her physically ill.

Sandi Decided to take Eileen's idea and Succeed in network marketing. She told herself, "No matter how long it takes, I will figure this out."

Sandi took on network marketing with a vengeance. The more she learned about the industry, the more excited she became. When Sandi agreed to join a company, she kept her business endeavors a secret from Ed. The secret did not last long. When Ed discovered Sandi's plans, he was angry. They fought constantly and even considered divorcing. Sandi stayed strong in her belief of herself and the industry.

The first four years in network marketing were awful for Sandi. She joined ten different companies. She went through a major learning curve.

Still, Sandi believed in the principles of network marketing. "Women are phenomenal with the gut intuition thinking," she says. For that reason, she refused to give up. She had seen, in her mind's eye, the success that could be hers. She kept looking for a company that fit her passion. She also spent time and energy in self-development. She intuitively knew she had to make personal changes to succeed in this industry of volunteer business partners.

She finally stumbled into the perfect company for her. They had products she was passionate about and ethical leadership she could support and who would support her as well. Sandi became one of the company's top distributors. Her Decision to Succeed paid off.

Sandi's WHY

To keep going when physical success is not visible takes a very strong WHY. Sandi had been to the top and had experienced the bottom. She knew she could weather both, but preferred the lifestyle of the rich and famous. The only viable option that would give her family the time and financial freedom she longed for was to own her own home-based business. The only way to be successful was to go on an extensive self-development program. Sandi devoured books, tapes and anything that would help her succeed. She found her mentors in the materials she eats up.

Sandi's Characteristics of a Great Company

From Sandi's extensive personal knowledge of different companies, she formulated a list of four characteristics that distinguish a great company:

1. The Product
According to Sandi, the product should be something that people would buy even if they did not earn an income from it. The majority of people are consumers instead of business builders. The product should also be consumable in order to promote repeat business.

2. The Company
A legitimate company should have experienced owners. Sandi advises people to assess the backgrounds of those at the corporate level. Know who they are, where they come

from and their background in network marketing as well as in traditional business. Doing so should be a great indication of the future stability of the company. It is also very important to read the company's policies and procedures before signing the contract. Make sure you are aware of what you're signing. "You would be shocked at some of the contracts people sign," said Sandi.

3. The Compensation Plan

There are at least four different types of compensation plans. People should choose based on three factors: how well they understand the plan, whether or not they fit well with the plan, and the financial opportunities provided by the plan. Everyone has different financial needs, so finding the right fit is important.

4. Timing

Companies should offer clear goals and strategies for success. Sandi says that prospects should figure out how much time is needed in order to achieve the kind of success they want.

Sandi's Ingredients for Success

After 16 years of experience in network marketing, Sandi now offers her recipes of success to beginners. She continues to learn and to tweak her own skills as necessary. Sandi says, "Being the best you can be means you never stop learning."

Her most valuable success ingredient is that network marketing is a relationship business. No one can be successful without helping others. **"When I talk to someone or meet someone for a cup of coffee, it is not about persuading them to join my business. It's about the friendship, and finding out what they are looking for,"** Sandi states. Successful home-based business entrepreneurs enjoy meeting and getting to know many different people.

Another success ingredient is to make a long-term commitment. Sandi advises, "At least three years of hard work are needed before substantial money can be made for most people." Sandi also says no one should enroll others without learning their reasons for making the commitment. Understand each person's goals and fears.

Finding a mentor within the same company is very beneficial. Should you be unable to find a company mentor, choose an author who has a clear plan for success. Sandi's mentor is Jim Rohn, an author and motivational speaker. She chose him because, in her eyes, he is a genius with years of experience.

Sandi also advises people to choose a sponsor wisely. People should not necessarily pick the first person who talks to them. Look instead for a reliable and motivated business partner.

Sandi's last success ingredient is to have confidence. She asserts, "Know that you have the passion and persistence. If there are others who have succeeded before, there is no reason why you cannot succeed also." Successful distributors must have a belief in the potential for success. To keep your belief strong you must enforce your skills with a self-development program.

Sandi's Strengths

When asked about her strengths, Sandi only comments on one: fortitude. She never gives up and keeps believing in the industry. According to her, the network marketing industry creates more millionaires than any other industry.

"My success lies in knowing, believing and understanding that with a home-based business, if you work consistently over a long time, you can succeed. The Key is to find like-minded people that you help succeed," she says.

Sandi's faith in the system keeps her strong. She relishes in the fact that network marketing does not require a remote office. With a cell phone or a computer, anyone, anywhere can succeed. This belief is what motivates Sandi to stay determined.

Sandi's Legacy

Sandi's legacy is to fight for the rights of others. Despite her outstanding success, Sandi never forgot her early financial troubles. She co-founded the Distributor Rights Association to protect the rights of individual independent contractors. She fights to preserve the right to make and keep residual income.

Sandi feels strongly about helping other women achieve financially freedom. She quotes, **"7 out of 10 women, in the USA, live in poverty. A home-based business is not an option, it is a necessity!"**

Sandi will always be a fantastic role model for women who want success in a home-based business or any business. She strives to make a difference every day. Sandi's true passion continues to be "Bringing the Mothers of America Home."

Sharon P. Davidson-Unkefer

Sharon's Background

Sharon P. Davidson-Unkefer was a joyous member of the
Women's Millionaire Club. I remember the day I asked to
interview her, her face lit up as she graciously said, "I'd be
honored to be included in such a prestigious group of
women." Before the book was completed, dear Sharon
passed away, on August 13, 2008, at the age of 68.

Sharon was a compassionate, magical woman. So magical, in
fact, that her grandson Sherman 'Shermie' Unkefer
nicknamed her "Magic Gal." Her family, husband, Sherman
Unkefer, III, sons Harley "Packy" Davidson, John Davidson,
Mark Davidson, Sean Davidson, their wives, and her
grandchildren, will always have fond memories of their
beloved mother and 'gramma.'

Sharon's happiest moments included spending time in her
custom cowboy resort, barbequing, listening to oldies, and
being surrounded by her family and friends. Her caring and
generous attitude is also reflected by the 13 pets that she
rescued and cared for - one was rescued within the two
weeks prior to her death.

People naturally flocked to Sharon for her sage advice and
folksy witticisms. Her spiritual roots flowed naturally from her
as she often quoted a scripture passage to soothe and aching

heart or lift a saddened spirit. One of her favorites was
Proverbs 31:25-30.

> She is clothed with strength and dignity; she can laugh
> at the days to come.
> She speaks with wisdom, and faithful instruction is on
> her tongue.
> She watches over the affairs of her household and
> does not eat the bread of idleness.
> Her children arise and call her blessed; her husband
> also, and he praises her:
> "Many women do noble things, but you surpass them
> all."
> Charm is deceptive, and beauty is fleeting; but a
> woman who fears the LORD is to be praised.

Her love of shopping was known by all. Her car automatically
knew the route to Costco, where Sharon, the "Queen of
Shopping," would breeze in to purchase not one, but 10 of
everything so she could frequently dispense gifts to her
children and grandchildren. Friends and family members
would frequently receive the odd coffeemaker, set of sheets,
movie or a comforter that matched their distinct personality.
Sharon would have a twinkle in her eye as she threw back her
head in laughter, knowing that she had surprised her
grandchild with a special treat they had not anticipated.

Sharon's inspirational work helped thousands of women find
the confidence to change their lives through owning a home-
based business. She spread light and joy when she entered a
room and her smile was infectious. Sharon and her husband,

Sherman, were their company's largest worldwide distributors.

Sharon's Strengths

Upon waking each morning, Sharon would head straight to her computer with her 10 fluffy dogs. Many days, she would find herself still in her pajamas in the middle of the afternoon as she feverishly collected ideas and notes to share in her next newsletter. She would stay up until the wee hours, writing a newsletter that she hoped would inspire her down-line. Sharon was an amazing woman with a special gift for nurturing. She spent long hours at her computer answering emails from distributors in the field that needed her help. She personally responded to all of her emails. Some folks needed more attention than others, and Sharon made the time to communicate with each person with encouraging words or thoughts.

Sharon was successful in her home-based business because she cared with all her heart about others. Her mission was to help others become successful. Sharon and Sherman were a team. He traveled and she stayed home. Her job was to care for, nurture and encourage team members – a role she took quite seriously. Team members were the recipients of her love and inspiration – from her newsletters to warm words of wisdom. Sharon often joked that Sherman was the "head" of their business, but she was the "neck," … "and everyone knows that the neck turns the head!"

Remembrances from Sharon's Loved Ones

"Sharon will be missed dearly. Her delightful, bright personality is an inspiration to all who have been blessed to meet her. I will never forget her beautiful smile. Sharon was truly special." – Gidget Giardino (Fort Lauderdale, FL)

"Sharon's newsletters were always eagerly anticipated and then shared with others. Her contributions made the world a better place." – Janet Callaway (Kamuela, HI)

"There are certain people who you come into contact with, and, from the moment you met them, you know they are special. You can't explain it – you just know that they come from a different mold. Sharon was one of those people. She was always happiest when she put others first. Now, as she is in a happier place, my thoughts and prayers are with her wonderful family. I feel blessed to have been able to call Sharon a friend, and I will truly miss her." – Ryan Anderson (Spanish Fork, UT)

"We should all be so grateful to have known such a loving, generous, enlightened, kindred spirit. Friends like these are far and few in-between, but being that kind of friend was Sharon's devotion in life. If all you had was a moment with her, she could make your day positive in an instant. Sharon was a blessing to my family. When my sister Laundy needed guidance, Sharon responded. I don't know how long I've known Sharon, but I have been around her long enough to see perfection.

To my sister Laundy: I know what it is like to have a second mother and a big sister. I wouldn't trade that for the world. Laundy, I see how you have also taken Sharon's example to become that spirit in my family. Laundy, I thank you for being that positive force in our lives. Thank you, Lord, for sending Sharon to be with us. Your grace is unyielding, as is your love." – Anthony, Adriana, and Talan Nido (Phoenix, AZ)

"The angels sang louder than ever when she came home to rest. Always in my prayers." – Suzanna Oberlies (Scottsdale, AZ)

"I have been blessed to know a woman who could brighten up a room with her smile, her stories, and her faith. May you find comfort in every hug you receive from those whom Sharon has touched." – Pegs Weber (Pell Lake, WI)

"Sharon was the absolute best mom, grandma, wife, mother-in-law and friend to all of us who have been privileged to have her in our lives. She has been my mom for the past 22 years, after I lost my mom at age 17. She was the grandma who poured rice on the kitchen floor for Markie and Luke, so that they could have a 'sandbox' to play in. I will never know a kinder, more generous person. Thank God for allowing her to be a part of my life. We will greatly miss you, Sharon – have some laughs with my mom, and we'll meet you in Heaven." – Cindy Davidson (Vista, CA)

"Sharon knew how nice it was to be important, but above all, she knew that it was important to be nice. She was always loving to everyone she met." – Eiji and Sariah Kakishita (Anaheim, CA)

"I was blessed to have her as my mother and my friend. My life will never be the same. I thank God and Savior Jesus Christ that we shall see each other again in paradise." – John Davidson (Scottsdale, AZ)

"What a loss to our company's family! However, our Heavenly Father knew her work here was done. She finished her race here on earth and has been received into the loving hands of our Heavenly Father for her reward. Sharon was a wonderful and beautiful servant of our Lord. She is now blessed." – Ruth and Harland Bohnee (Tempe, AZ)

"I considered Sharon one of the best friends I have ever known. Having her as my friend was a great pleasure. She was not only beautiful on the inside and outside, but she was also loving, compassionate, passionate, and fun. She taught me many lessons on how to be generous, forgiving, and strong in my Christian faith. I'm going to miss her terribly." – Deborah Burns (Phoenix, AZ)

"Sharon was the most inspirational, spiritual, and loving woman I have ever known. She was the first to step up and hold out a hand to lift someone up who was down; the first to laugh at a bad joke; the first to come to your defense if you were being treated unfairly; and the first to tell you the truth, even if you didn't want to hear it. Truth, honesty, and integrity were her greatest attributes. She dearly loved her family, friends, and all of God's creatures, especially her dogs. When Sharon was on vacation with her family in Alaska, a baby bear that had been separated from its mother wandered into the campgrounds. Sharon was told by the locals that the baby bear would not survive on its own, so Sharon spent the remainder of her vacation trying to find someone who would come to the camp and rescue the bear. After that trip, I gave her the title of "Mama Bear." I will miss you, Mama Bear. I am a better person for having known you and loved you." – Sandy DiGiovanni (Huntington Beach, CA)

"Time goes on, even though I don't want it to. I know that most grandmas are those special people that granddaughters get to see on special occasions and memorable moments and those weekend trips. My Gramma Sharon, on the other hand, was not just my grandma. She was like a second mom to me. She got to see me almost seven days a week for the last four years. She was there when I got accepted into the high school my mom had dreamed of me going to, she was there through the different dances and prom, she was there through the dating scene, and she was there all the days in between. I always knew that when I got home from school my grandma would be at her desk. As soon as I walked in, she would say, "Alexa, honey, how's your day?" and I would tell her everything, whether it was good or bad. This year, my first year of college, will be harder than I though. My Gramma Sharon, after countless attempts to try and make

231

me take this first year off, finally realized that I was going to college, was going to move out on my own, and this would be the first year she wouldn't get to see me everyday like that past four years of high school. But I promised her that I would make weekly visits and that she could come and stay with me at my apartment whenever she wanted. She never did get to see the apartment and didn't even get to hear about my first day of school. I know that people say we should all be happy that her suffering is over and that she is in a better place, but the truth is that I never imagined there would be a day when I didn't see her or talk to her. I never thought she would be gone, even after she got sick. Now she is gone and I've lost one of the best people in my life. I know that she is better off in heaven, it is just hard to let go. I love you Gramma!" – Alexa Unkefer (Tempe, AZ)

"I needed a little time to pass before I could write about my mom. It's so cool to read all the nice things people have written and how much she meant to everyone. I was so fortunate to have her for a mom. We never really had a dad, but with my mom you didn't really need one. She would sometimes feel sad or guilty about that, but we always told her she was the best mom and dad anyone would ever want. A lot of kids we grew up with had these stiff, stuffy traditional households, but our house was always way off the beaten path and everybody loved it and felt at home with my mom. She was so kind and generous to everyone she met. When you met my mom you got the real deal and within ten minutes you loved her. She could socialize with big shots and our blue collar biker friends and everyone left smiling and

232

saying, "Your mom is really great!" She was. I talked with her every day. She was an early riser like me, and she'd often talk with me on my morning commute for well over an hour. We'd just laugh and talk about everything. I sure miss that, and this has been the longest time that I haven't talked to her. It's rough. I was so fortunate to spend the last couple of years with her, doing all the landscape work and spending so much time just being with her. It's like God knew, and he wanted her to be happy before she had to go. I just want to end this by saying how much I love my mom and there's a special place in the yard that her and I would talk and share things early in the morning, even when she was sick, and I'm glad I was able to build that for you, mom. I love my brothers and want to thank everyone who was there when mom needed them, you know who you are and you are angels and I will never forget your kindness and strength. See you Ma."
- Mark Davidson (Vista, CA)

Sharon's Legacy

Sharon's legacy will always be the generous heart and love she spread to her beloved family, especially her grandchildren. That love flowed to everyone who came within 10 feet of this gracious lady and extended around the world.

Sharon published a popular newsletter that provided advice and acknowledged accomplished distributors. Through her love and kindness, Sharon touched the lives of many people, especially women, around the world. Her newsletters and kind words of praise will long be remembered by the tens of thousands whose lives she touched.

One of Sharon's Favorite Poems

Sharon spent hours combing over her numerous collections of poems to find the exact right one to start each newsletter. This was one of her favorites.

> *"As we grow up, we learn that even the one person that wasn't supposed to ever let you down probably will.*
> *You will have your heart broken probably more than once, and it's harder every time.*
> *You'll break hearts too, so remember how it felt when yours was broken.*
> *You'll fight with your best friend.*
> *You'll blame a new love for things an old one did.*
> *You'll cry because time is passing too fast, and you'll eventually lose someone you love.*
> *So, take too many pictures, laugh too much, and love like you've never been hurt, because every sixty seconds you spend upset is a minute of happiness, you'll never get back.*
> *Don't be afraid that your life will end. Be afraid it will never begin. Live simply.*
> *Love generously.*
> *Care deeply.*
> *Speak kindly.*
> *Leave the rest to God."*

Doni Smith

Doni's Background

Doni Smith's life dramatically changed from her experiences in network marketing. She met the love of her life, husband Larry. She achieved financial freedom. And she took control of her own time. This incredible story shows how a young woman can reach her dreams through network marketing.

Doni's story begins as a young girl, watching her mother unsuccessfully test out numerous network marketing companies. Doni did not want to continue on this career path. She paved her own path by joining the corporate world, believing corporations were more secure.

Corporate life was difficult, especially when her company downsized. Doni quickly discovered, "I was trading time for money. Somebody else owned me. I did not own my own time. I was kept from my full potential."

As a single parent, she had to be very creative. Babysitting and other odd jobs helped her put food on the table. During a period of economic strain, more people had been laid off. Many over-qualified people were vying for the same jobs. Doni saw her options slipping away.

As a loving parent, her first concern was her children. "I felt like my children should not have to suffer because I got laid off. It wasn't their fault. That's when I realized I could not trade time for money, because I would give 50% of my paycheck for someone else to take care of my children. I needed a way to make as much money as possible in certain designated time slots. Parenting was first," Doni recalls. She was desperate to make money and cared deeply for her children.

When Doni confided in her pastor, he brought up the idea of network marketing. Doni was skeptical at first, as she had never met anyone who was successful in the industry. Her attitude changed when her situation became dire: "The lady I was babysitting for was working 40 to 70 hours a week. She said, 'I don't need you anymore, because I have decided to take back my time and give myself freedom. I am going to go full board with this network marketing concept.'" Out of financial desperation, Doni was forced into her pastor's living room to give network marketing a chance. The risk ended up being a blessing in disguise.

When Doni jumped into network marketing, she had a lot to learn. Although she was not a smashing success from the beginning, she **stayed committed to the learning process.** She remembers, "I had a very big learning curve. The biggest challenge for me was **personal development**, because I had been so upset with where I was in life that people could see the despair in my face. I was not what you would call a shining light." She had to become **more attractive to people** so that they would be willing to listen to her share information about her product.

How did Doni stay motivated to learn? She considered the alternative – going back to the painful situation she had previously struggled with. **Her WHY was strong enough to help her persevere and to push through the learning curve.**

What was Doni's WHY? She needed to feed her two beautiful children. Paying the electricity bill and the rent were Doni's immediate concerns. In the long run, she had other motives: "I did not want to see my children go through what I had been through. In that period, I relied on food stamps. It was very humbling, but I looked at my children and knew that I did not want them to feel that way. I knew that if I did not make a change, then they too would be subjected to this pain." Doni's love for her children and her determination to provide a **better lifestyle with more opportunities** kept her strong.

Through network marketing, Doni also met her future husband Larry Smith. Today, the couple lives together and works together. They live a dream lifestyle with financial stability and control of their own time. With six children and two grandchildren, Doni's family is the ultimate network marketing family.

Doni Decided to Succeed

Doni's decision to start in on her new home-based business path was a difficult one at first. The lingering fears of watching her mother struggle to achieve minimal success still haunted her. She **Decided** the only way to Succeed was to "dive into network marketing." Even though Doni was scared to make that important decision, she dramatically changed her life by making that choice.

As part of the learning curve, Doni took several steps toward achieving success.

1. Submerge in the Learning Process

Doni instinctively knew she needed massive personal development. She became 'teachable' and soaked up every morsel of information that would move her business forward. She quickly learned that a distributor can spend hours and hours learning about the product, but doing so does not bring in a paycheck. So, Doni set aside daily 'learning time,' but spent her 'prime-time' moments taking action.

2. Get into Action by Talking

When she began, Doni felt physically ill at the thought of initiating conversations with strangers. She was petrified by the idea of asking people to grant her some time, let alone sell anything to them. That was when she thought about feeding her children, and she became motivated. She learned to take advantage of the **slivers of time that she could work her business.**

Doni started with her warm market – her mother's past clients. To get over her **fear of talking to people**, Doni engaged in conversations while on errands. "**My purpose was to meet and greet as many people as possible. In the time I allocated to finding new people, I literally went door**

to door. I went to business owners. That was uncomfortable," Doni remembers. Between grand openings and job fairs, she **seized every opportunity to engage with people**. By habitually meeting new people, Doni created her own warm market.

3. Be in Revenue Producing Time
Revenue producing time was not the time to be learning or studying. Revenue Producing Time was 'talk time.' Doni filled her schedule with appointments to talk to people directly, either in person or over the phone. She then **sorted through the yes's and no's in the time** she had put aside.

4. Learn a Simple Script
To help her introduce the topic of network marketing, Doni created a basic script to use when she met new people. She said, "**Hi, there's something I want to show you. You may not be interested, but it will only take me 15 minutes.**" In a mere 15 minutes she could help a person change their life. If they did not want or need her service, she knew she had given her best and could cheerfully move on to the next person.

5. Follow Up
The script enabled Doni to set up one-on-one meetings with new customers. In these meetings, she listened and learned about what the people wanted from the business opportunity.

Doni's Ingredients for Success

Doni's system has helped many new distributors prosper. The top five ingredients she passes along to others are quite simple.

1. Field Training

As a proponent of field training, Doni works with new consultants so they may earn while they learn. They set up an individualized game plan together, based on their time freedom. Doni knows that some people have more time to devote to the business than others.

2. Personalize Based on the Person's WHY

Doni always modifies the plan based on each person's goals. She asks the client: "What do you want to get out of the business?" Doni believes that each plan should vary based on the individual.

3. Give the Person Basic Fundamentals

Doni assists each person in reaching their goals by helping them obtain the basic skills necessary for success.

4. Mentor

Doni strives to be a supportive and helpful coach through the initial steps.

5. Help to Duplicate the Process

Doni knows that when a person can duplicate the process on his or her own, the system is complete.

Doni's Strengths

Doni's painful experiences emboldened her and helped her to relate to other women. She can empathize with others and say, "I have felt that way." The ability to relate with other people has allowed Doni to build solid relationships.

During her years of experience, Doni learned to **cultivate better people skills and to become a better listener.** "If you are a good listener, you can deliver better information. If your information is not relevant to the individual, then relaying that information is pointless. You are not doing them justice, so you are only wasting your time and theirs," she advises. One of her most useful tools is her ability to listen carefully to others.

Another of Doni's strengths is her **perseverance to overcome any obstacle.** Change is frightening for most people, which is why Doni's determination is empowering to others.

Doni's WHY

Doni's WHY is constantly growing and changing. In the beginning, her WHY was financial desperation and making sure the bills were paid. Her children were always a major part of her WHY. Doni wants to set an example for her children and to show them how to **think outside of the box.**

While most people believe that the only option available is the corporate ladder, Doni wants to show that there are other ways to succeed.

Doni's WHY has developed into a broader idea on a larger scale. "I have realized that I can not only touch my children's lives but others' lives as well. I can empower many people. Now **my WHY is, 'How many lives can I touch? I've realized a little success, so I can focus on helping others do the same,"** says Doni.

Doni's Legacy

Doni's children continue to be her first priority. Her goal is to **empower them to be all that God has designed them to be**. Doni wants her legacy to be a gift to her children, so that they have the financial resources to accomplish their dreams. "**I come from a long line of 'career strugglers.' I am glad that it stopped with me. I have empowered myself, and I can empower others. My home-based business changed the entire direction of my family. My children have experienced their mother's success and they will pass success on to their children and grandchildren. The Success Trajectory of our family has been changed forever**," she declares. Doni has already accomplished that goal by giving strength to her children and to numerous other people around the world.

Sherrie Olp

Sherrie's Background

Sherrie Olp has come a long way from her Iowa family roots. Still, she appreciates her Midwest background, which she says gave her a great work ethic. As a child, Sherrie learned the family values that she has taken with her into adulthood.

From an early age, even though Sherrie knew that her parents' marriage struggled, she understood the importance of family. She knew that she wanted a different life. **"I believe in walking through doors that are open. As a door opens, an opportunity becomes available. I learned not to fear these opportunities, to walk through doors that open to me and see where they lead. I have done that all through my life**," Sherrie says. As she was determined to improve her situation, Sherrie seized every opportunity available.

Sherrie worked her way up in business. Starting as a bookkeeper, and progressing up the ladder into financial management, she eventually became CFO of the company. She enjoyed the daily challenges, making business happen, and creating a foundation for her company. The non-fulfilling part was doing this for someone else's business. That was when she saw the possibilities in network marketing. She says, **"Network marketing is very non-judgmental. For only a few dollars, anyone can start a business, work hard, and develop it into whatever they want it to be. We know that not everyone wants to do this. Some people just want a** social outlet or a hobby. Network marketing is not for everybody, but what I like is the unlimited possibilities." That possibility is what enabled the little girl from Iowa to become an inspiration figure in the home-based business world.

Sherrie Decided to Succeed

Unlike many women who became millionaires through network marketing, Sherrie did have a background in business. She and her husband own a construction business, and their livelihood has always depended on how hard they worked. Because she had a job, and children still in school to care for, Sherrie started part time in network marketing to test the waters. Because she was excited to see how much money she could make in the industry, she very quickly threw herself into the new business completely.

Sherrie quickly learned how much fun she could have in network marketing. "It's been a blast to know that **you can design network marketing how you want**. I don't like restrictions or boundaries. What works for me may not work for someone else. **Network marketing is about who you are, including your background, your skill set, your goals, and creating something from nothing**," she says. She truly enjoyed **helping people succeed using their strengths and talents**. One person's success does not take away from another person's success. Everyone can win. This thrilling idea inspired Sherrie to pursue network marketing further.

Although Sherrie was excited about network marketing, she felt apprehensive about leaving the comfort zone of her stable job. She felt insecure about leaving a steady income from a firm she had been with for 15 years.

Sherrie also immediately felt the pressure of selling. Initially, she had a fear of asking for sales and "closing the deal." "We want network marketing to be a natural outcome of our passion and love of what we do. I learned that **people want to be led**. I had to learn to lead them through the products and recommend the program that would best meet their needs," she says. Once Sherrie overcame her fears, she quickly flourished in her network marketing business.

Sherrie's Strengths

Sherrie attributes her success to two key strengths. The first is a **competitive edge**. She **loves challenges** and always strives to do her best. "I am more than a little competitive, which is probably a **natural inclination. If someone is going to win, it's going to be me**. I will not only do the job, but I will do it well. **It's not about running over people, but it's about doing the job to the best of my abilities**," she says. This engrained competitiveness helped Sherrie to push to the top.

The second key strength is Sherrie's outstanding people skills. Even though some were **natural** to her, Sherrie is continually learning new skills. **She learned to ask questions, listen closely, and alter her intentions accordingly**. She **listens and**

helps people unlock their personal desires. Using these people skills, Sherrie identifies with each person and adjusts to their individual needs.

Sherrie's Ingredients for Success

Coaching and training people are Sherrie's main ingredients for network marketing. Her advice is to help people learn and follow these baby steps:

1. Love the Work

Sherrie emphasizes hooking up with a **company that you love**. A love of what you do is the most important factor in success.

2. Be Authentic

According to Sherrie, there is a major difference between selling a product and genuinely standing behind the product. Be sure that the product you sell is a good match for you.

3. Be Consistent

As network marketing is open and unstructured, manage your business activities well. Sherrie knows this may be difficult for people who have many work and personal obligations, but **consistent daily activity** is the best way to reach your potential.

4. Be Persistent

Sometimes, you may see great results immediately. Other times, you may not. Sherrie promotes staying persistent, and she says to keep working every day. Although this may be difficult if you do not see immediate results, time and persistence will eventually lead to success.

5. Share Your Knowledge
Teaching others well by being the expert in your field is a strategy of Sherrie's. She stresses having a working knowledge of the products and the business. You have to be able to "teach your downline to teach" in order to succeed.

6. Show How to Duplicate
Provide other people with step-by-step instructions on how to succeed in network marketing by duplicating a successful process. A simple system is critical to your success.

Sherrie's WHY

When Sherrie first started in network marketing, her WHY was **to be in control of her life and business while still earning a steady income.** She wanted to be in charge. As she grows older, Sherrie's WHY is to **create a retirement income that is not based on the ups and downs of the economy.** In this way, she will be in control of her retirement years as well.

Sherrie's Legacy

With her husband Tom and her sons, Travis and Trevor, Sherrie's family is a supportive and caring group. Sherrie's family is most important to her. "**We enjoy funding family events, so that extended family can come to spend time**

together and not worry about affordability. The legacy of having her children and their children stay close to their cousins and aunts and uncles through the years to come, sharing wonderful family moments together. I think that is beautiful!" she says. Her legacy will be the close, loving family that she helped to create.

Carolyn Johnson

Carolyn's Background

Before Carolyn Johnson became a millionaire through network marketing, she was very content in the corporate world. She loved her job. She was living the American Dream, so she thought. She was a single mom of two adult children. Her daughter Cathy was finishing college and her son Tommy was finishing high school. With little warning, her beloved corporate industry started to change. Carolyn was forced to change as well.

With an uncertain path in front of her, Carolyn jumped into her own business, a 'cause-related marketing' venture under the umbrella of a gentleman capitalist. Through her work, Carolyn helped to benefit children's hospitals around the country. Unfortunately, the gentleman who ran the umbrella company was dishonest, so funds were depleted very quickly. Carolyn had to find a new path once again.

Carolyn started her own consulting marketing business because of her corporate experience. She had a passion for startup companies and wrote business plans and marketing plans for them. When small companies faced trouble, she analyzed the employees to determine where they might feel most valued. This new job gave Carolyn momentary hope, but very little income.

Carolyn faced even more serious challenges. Startup companies experiencing financial problems would not always pay her fully or on time. She quickly learned that a startup company with little capital put her fees at the bottom of the "to pay" list. Without the corporate benefits she was accustomed to, life became a struggle for Carolyn.

In a last ditch attempt to regain her financial footing, Carolyn orchestrated and executed a major event in April 2000, hoping to raise enough capital to make the event an annual one. Instead of providing the income she anticipated, it left her over $100,000 in debt.

With no 401k, no viable income, and drowning in debt, she had to make some depressing changes in her life. Instead of taking the bankruptcy route, she chose to be responsible for her financial situation. "After feeling sorry for myself, I sold my home and gave everything away, except those most memorable items that I could not replace. I moved in with a friend to a 10 by 12 foot room, which was a humbling experience as a 58 year old," Carolyn recalls. By December of 2000, she felt trapped in a downward spiral of debt.

Carolyn Decided to Succeed

Sensing she had hit rock bottom, Carolyn made a Decision to change her future. She put together a ten-year plan and opened her mind to all new business opportunities.

Back in 1970, she had been introduced to network marketing by her cousin while having lunch with him. Carolyn was still flying high in corporate America, so she immediately dismissed his business opportunity. "I was taught to get a job, work hard, get a raise, and work harder. This was supposed to be the American dream. I did not understand residual income or the power of duplication," she says. She thought her cousin was into some kind of 'get rich quick' scheme. She had judged him harshly, thinking, "Why doesn't he go out and get a real job?"

Fast forward to after writing her ten-year plan, when Carolyn and her children were invited to a family reunion hosted by the same cousin in November 2000. Her mouth dropped as she saw, smelled and touched his extravagant lifestyle. Over the next couple of years her cousin, Bob, became the brother and mentor she had never had. When he contracted cancer, the two became even closer. While Carolyn and Bob stayed close throughout his fight for his life, he softly and quietly re-introduced her to the network marketing opportunity. Carolyn realized his home-based business had provided his lavish lifestyle. Carolyn was enamored with his wonderful life. She **Decided** she, too, could have this lifestyle. Carolyn trusted Bob to be her mentor and coach as he helped her start a career in network marketing.

Carolyn knew enough to know that **success could not happen overnight. At least two or three years are needed to build any business.** Therefore, she made a promise to her cousin to stay committed to the business for two years. **She vowed**

to be coachable, consistent, and never to quit. This promise ended up being one of the best Carolyn ever made.

Carolyn's Ingredients for Success

1. Purpose
Carolyn knows that nothing happens without purpose. She advises everyone to have a goal and the drive to achieve that goal.

2. Learning Curve
With any business, there is a learning curve. Learning all of the skills necessary for success can sometimes take a long time.

3. Treat Network Marketing Like a Business
Some people have a lazy approach and give up after trying for a short time. Carolyn, on the other hand, never treated her business as a hobby. Instead, if a person was not interested in her business offer or product, **Carolyn made the decision not to let that refusal be a deciding factor in her future.**

4. Coach Others
Carolyn says, "Your own success only comes when you can teach and mentor other people to be successful."

5. Success as a Team
Success is dependent on the assistance and guidance of your team. "I knew I was going to be successful when I helped others become successful," Carolyn says.

6. Educate Yourself

Carolyn continues to read books by leaders in the industry. She knows people like Donald Trump, Robert Kiyosaki, David Bach, Dr. Tom Barret, and Warren Buffet can provide great insight into how to attain success.

7. Create a Plan

When someone is struggling from paycheck to paycheck, they do not plan for the future. Carolyn strives to help these less fortunate people create a long-term "plan B."

8. Have Hope

When Carolyn started to achieve success, she nearly forgot to dream. When you struggle just to survive, dreaming becomes something only children do. "I believe that this business gives us the opportunity to put hope back into our lives and to dream again," she says.

The Benefits of being a Woman

Carolyn understands the hardships that women face in the corporate world. Only 16% of the people in top positions are women. Carolyn's approach is to combine the assets from both men and women. **Women, she says, approach business in a loving and feeling way**. Men, on the other hand, are more pragmatic. They think more about making money and the risks involved in a business endeavor. "Look at it from both perspectives. Take the wonderful things of being a woman, but lead with a business opportunity in mind," she says. Her goal is to educate more women on this principle and to help them move out of the poverty mindset.

Carolyn's WHY

Carolyn remembers the first time her network marketing coach asked her about her intended monthly income. She quickly spat out, "$5,000 a month." Bob didn't respond quickly, and fearing the amount was too high, she said, "I just need enough to make my monthly payments with a little left over for savings." Her cousin asked, **"Why not $50,000? A doctor may earn a high income, but he is not smarter than you. He just studied differently."** She was astonished. Carolyn quickly realized that a network marketer must study like a doctor in order to be good at the job. She took on the challenge.

Carolyn's Legacy

Carolyn's legacy is her beloved family. By experiencing financial and time freedom, Carolyn has been a role model for her children and their children. Carolyn is fortunate to have six beautiful grandchildren. "My grandchildren will enjoy income from what I am doing for decades to come," she says proudly.

Carolyn's other legacy will be her charitable efforts. Her goal is to tithe $1 million to several programs by the year 2012. She will always be remembered for her efforts to give back to her family, her team, and her community.

Joyce Dell

Joyce's Background

'Let freedom ring,' is Joyce Dell's motto. She loves her financial and time freedom as a network marketer. Along with her loving husband Norm, she travels, plays golf, snorkels, and rides bikes. They split their time between the United States and Canada, where part of Joyce's family lives. This exciting lifestyle is possible because of Joyce's extraordinary success in network marketing.

Joyce's professional career began in interior design. For many years, Joyce designed offices for clients. "That is a profession in which, if I was selling a house or working with a client, I had a job. When I finished the job, I was unemployed," she remembered. The income was not steady, so Joyce decided to change directions.

Joyce and her husband bought a Burger King restaurant in Santa Barbara, California. They expanded and invested in three more fast food restaurants. Although the businesses were successful, Joyce and her husband were unhappy and worked long hours. Her only mission was to have the freedom to travel, but they could not leave the restaurant for more than three days at a time. They felt trapped and tied down. Another problem was that they did not want their livelihoods left in the hands of teenagers. For these reasons, the couple sold the restaurants and decided to take a different course.

Joyce Decided to Succeed

Before being a distributor, **Joyce was a product user. She had been introduced to some exceptional products, which she loved.** Then, the couple temporarily returned to Canada, because her mother-in-law was ill. That was when Joyce discovered that the company was expanding into the Canadian marketplace.

Joyce was looking for something to fill her time and she thought that sharing these products with others would be a great option. She **Decided** to make her business lucrative, so she could travel around the continent and do her work. **"That is the most fabulous thing about network marketing,"** she says, **"It is portable. We have business all over the world. It's not because we know people all over the world, but because people know other people. We are global. We are in 47 different countries."** This international opportunity enabled Joyce to fulfill her dream of traveling and to achieve financial freedom in the process.

Joyce was fortunate to find a ground floor opportunity in a company that had a solid foundation. Still, she knows that not everyone is as lucky. "Understand that there are hills and valleys that never stop. Keep doing what you are doing. Keep calling. Keep putting yourself out there. Never quit. Your time will come," Joyce says encouragingly to new prospects. Even without the kind of foundation that Joyce had, success is possible for anyone who makes an effort.

Joyce's Strengths

According to Joyce, all of her strengths are learned. She developed some important strengths in network marketing, but others were a result of her upbringing. Her father, for example, was a people person. He taught Joyce to be friendly and personable. Joyce even enjoys meeting new people on airplanes, and she credits this ability to her father's teachings. "I travel a lot. When I am boarding, I stand at the front of the airplane and look out at the people. I choose to sit by the person who smiles at me first," Joyce says. **The ability to enjoy being around people is a learned skill.**

Joyce's stubbornness taught her never to quit. She attributes her excellent drive and determination to her experience in network marketing. Over time, she acquired the ability to stay focused and to persevere. That characteristic is hugely important for success in any business.

Joyce's WHY

Freedom was always Joyce's WHY, but the type of freedom has changed over time. In the beginning, Joyce was looking for the freedom to work with the people of her choice. She relished in the freedom of managing her own time. "I do not sleep in. I trust my body clock and never consider an alarm clock," she claims.

Now that she is growing older, freedom has a different meaning for Joyce. Her WHY is about the freedom to spend time with her family. She appreciates every minute with her grandchildren: "I have wonderful grandchildren who I love to spend time with. We enjoy going on trips. Soon, they will be too old for Disneyland." After 18 years in the business, Joyce has other priorities that require her time.

Joyce's Ingredients for Success

Joyce follows an eleven step program for success:

1. Keep the Plan Simple

Joyce believes that simplicity is key. "The plan should be simple and easy to follow," she says. Once you start to complicate the plan, you will face problems.

2. Learn

As you move through the plan, continue to learn. Keep an open mind and soak in any new information as you progress through the business. The more you learn, the faster you work and progress.

3. Have Confidence

All distributors need confidence in the company and products. To ensure you can meet those needs, Joyce advises others to find a company that fits with their needs and that they can genuinely support.

4. Make Visits
To learn more about the company, Joyce visits the company headquarters. She meets the president and CEO of the company to gain a better impression of the management.

5. Use the Product
Joyce shows her confidence in the product by being a regular user. Other people see that she stands behind her statements and that she truly loves the product.

6. Create a Team
Joyce contributes most of her success to surrounding herself with a strong team. This is what many in the corporate world do not understand," Joyce states. In order to be successful, build a network of dedicated and supportive people.

7. Do the Work
If you put effort into your business, your team will show even more support. "If people are willing to work, I attach myself to their hips. I talk to them four or five times a day, because I want to be with them," Joyce says.

8. Get Started
The most common mistake is that people try to learn everything before beginning a career in network marketing. Joyce argues that the best strategy is to jump right in. With the Internet, all of the information is at our fingertips. She tells others that they should not feel trapped by the urge to learn everything about the company and the product.

9. Set Goals

Joyce learned firsthand the benefits of setting clear goals. At first, she only set long-term goals and never short-term goals. She never reached those goals, so she did not understand the advantages of goal setting. She recalls, "I had the goals in my head, but I did not always write them on paper. When I did, there was a major leap in my business. I can't say enough about writing goals on paper." Even if you don't believe that writing down your goals will help you, try to do so anyways.

10. Be Coachable

Follow the system that has already worked for others. **The kiss of death is to try to succeed your own way by reinventing the wheel.**

11. Practice

Practice is the only way to perfect your skills. For Joyce, speaking in public was a petrifying experience. "I had such a fear of public speaking that the first time I had to stand up to do a three minute introduction of my sponsor, I actually had an out-of-body experience. I was huffing and puffing and gasping for air," Joyce remembers. She managed to conquer this fear by practicing at home with her family. Over time, she eventually felt more comfortable speaking in front of crowds.

Joyce's Legacy

Joyce most important contributions are to her family. Her main goal in life is "to be a loving, caring wife, stepmother, grandmother, and friend." The beautiful family that Joyce helped build will be her greatest legacy.

With her incredible success, Joyce also hopes to enrich the lives of others as well. Joyce hopes to **leave the world a better place** and **to help people feel good about who they are**. Too many people feel that there is some lid that holds them down. She refers to a quote by John Maxwell: "Leaders are lid lifters." For Joyce, **a leader is one who can lift up those lids to help people bloom and grow**. Her ability to be a fantastic leader has already helped millions of people around the world.

Dianne Leavitt

Dianne's Background

Dianne Leavitt raised four wonderful sons and continues to be an active mother, with two of her sons still living at home. She is happily married and lives in a newly remodeled house. Although Dianne lives a dream life today, she had to deal with many hardships to reach this point.

Dianne always had a knack for business and was confident in her ability to accomplish great things. She started working at a Hallmark store when she was 15 years old. At a young age, Dianne got married and had children. Because she wanted to stay at home with her small children, Dianne became a piano teacher. Life became extremely difficult, as Dianna struggled to make ends meet. Her troubles peaked when she and her husband divorced. "I was 24 years old, and I was scared. I was divorced, alone, and inexperienced," Dianne recalls. Her family was far away and could not give much reassurance. With young children to care for, Dianne needed to make money fast.

Dianne considered waitressing, but she quickly realized that all of her income would be spent on childcare. As a naïve young adult, Dianne was embarrassed and lost. She felt trapped. When Dianne's brother introduced her to network marketing, she was initially opposed to the idea. However, she agreed to attend a presentation on the principles of network marketing. Dianne figured out a plan beforehand –

to fold her arms and endure the presentation and then to forget about the presentation afterwards.

From the moment that Dianne walked into the door of the presentation, her plan crumbled. As she listened attentively to the discussion, she was captivated by the concept of building wealth. "The idea that all people could enable themselves if they tried was what excited me," she recalls. "I believed certain principles. They are accurate principles witnessed all over the place. **I decided to get involved.**" Dianne's brother was shocked by her immediate passion.

Shortly after the presentation, Dianne received her first paycheck of $36.63. For most people, that amount is not much. Through her eyes, however, that paycheck significantly increased her budget. She was ecstatic and felt driven to keep trying.

Through her hard work, Dianne became a leader in the company. Her measly checks soon jumped to over $6,000. "I was so filled with gratitude and bewilderment. **Network marketing was a vehicle that enabled me to become bigger than my circumstances,**" she reflects. Today, Dianne is happily married and lives a fabulous lifestyle with her husband and children.

Dianne Decided to Succeed

Dianne tool several steps to propel her into success. First, she believed in herself. Her naivety emboldened her to take on the challenge. "I was so young. I did not know I couldn't," she says. "It was that naivety." That innocence helped instill a belief that she could succeed no matter what.

Dianne also found her vehicle to success - **network marketing**. In the network marketing industry, she could work from home and earn an income while caring for her children.

Once Dianne had a belief in herself and a vehicle for success, the next step was a belief in the vehicle. She stayed disciplined and adhered to the system. Her faith in network marketing grew stronger as she saw more and more results.

The fourth and final step was to focus on the WHY. Dianne had her own personal reason to keep trying when times were tough: the need to provide security for her family. That WHY enabled Dianne to endure tough times.

Dianne's Ingredients for Success

1. Change with the Times
The system for marketing has changed over the past decade. With technological advancements, communication continues to change drastically. "Technology has changed. Information has changed. The way we interact with people has changed. The medium of communication is completely different," she maintains. Changing with the times is necessary to make a massive difference in today's world.

2. Keep it Simple

Following a simple process is important. "I feel there are certain truths in this industry that everyone has to follow," she says. "Certain things work, and certain things don't." Follow those simple procedures that have worked for other people. The basic principles of network marketing are not complex, so anyone can implement and share them. Many people, including Dianne, **cling to simple things**. Keep the system simple to help others succeed.

3. Have the Desire to Help

Dianne's finds motivation in her desire to help others. She enjoys seeing others fulfill their dreams.

4. Keep Your Focus

When she faces challenges, Dianne concentrates on the next step. "It is never wise to look over your shoulder, because it will scare you to death. Keep your focus," she advises.

5. Stay Loyal

An important aspect of success is to stay loyal to the company and the product. The key is to learn as much as possible about the products and compensation plan. "I am a ferocious defender of what I think is right and good. I am loyal to the cause, but the cause must be worthy of standing behind. That is the prerequisite for me. If the morals and the integrity of the enterprise match my integrity, then I can sell it," Dianne states. Show your loyalty by participating in the opportunities that your company offers. Attend meetings and conferences to stay active within the company.

6. Show Off

Dianne's attitude is that she is not selling, but showing off. The standards of the company and product must be extremely high. With a company that has wonderful principles backing her up, Dianne feels invincible.

7. Share Your Story

Get your message out by talking to anyone who will listen. Don't bet everything on one distributor. Become a great communicator by sharing your story with numerous people. The story should be personal and specific so that people can relate and feel a connection with you.

8. Understand and Empower

Dianne has slowly realized that not everyone had the immediate passion that she felt. Over time, she learned to transfer her passion to other people. In this way, she could help them feel the joy of personal success.

The key is to empower others instead of doing their work for them. In the beginning, Dianne struggled when she wanted success for others more than they wanted the success for themselves. She disabled herself by doing work for others. She had to take on a new strategy.

Dianne learned to leverage others by spreading her passion. "When you're a leader, that means managing a huge mass of people and helping them to become better," she says. "I love that part of the job. It's really one of the great benefits of network marketing. By helping other people become better and achieve their goals, you grow yourself and become a better person." Dianne became an incredible leader by helping herself first and then transferring her passion to others.

The Benefits of Being a Woman

For Dianne, women have so many choices. Her advice to women is, "Dare to hope. Dare to try. Dare to believe. Dare to educate yourself, and have an open mind to make yourself and your family better. Trust yourself." Women can help themselves by helping others. Dianne says that women naturally have strength, and network marketing is based on sharing that strength with others. Dianne's hope is to "create security, peace, and an environment of giving." With network marketing, women can become free.

Dianne's WHY

Dianne's WHY has always been an extension of her personal fears. In the beginning, her WHY was to **protect her children** and to pay the bills. She was so petrified that her financial fears defined her as a person.

Recently, Dianne's WHY has transformed by encompassing larger reasons. She has a desire to help as many people as possible, because her fear is being alone. "I wish I could help more people. Frankly, not many people have my lifestyle. If I can't share and experience that with others, it's lonely," she says.

Dianne's Legacy

Dianne's legacy will always be her amazing contributions to her company. She did her part to **help the company reach its highest potential**. "I have been so blessed that the only proper thing to do is **to give back to the company**," she says. In the process, she enables other people to reach their personal goals. Dianne will always be remembered for the charisma, energy, and enthusiasm that she brings to the company.

Marilyn and Sarah Stewart

Marilyn and Sarah's Backgrounds

Marilyn and Sarah Stewart are a mother-daughter team from Albert, Canada. Marilyn is the mother of three beautiful daughters, including Sarah. At nine weeks of age, Sarah developed health problems, which precipitated Marilyn's search for holistic solutions. She discovered fantastic health products through network marketing companies and started using them in her 30's. As a consumer, she never thought that the company she is with today would launch her into millionaire status.

Only ten years ago, Marilyn was juggling five different jobs. Between being a teacher and a mom, Marilyn feared that she was balancing too many responsibilities. She felt limited in the education system and always looked for bigger opportunities.

Marilyn saw many other teachers taking on second jobs to stay afloat. When Sarah wanted to attend university in the United States, Marilyn considered network marketing as a full-time job. The industry provided so **many possibilities for income**. Marilyn was hoping to earn an extra $2,000 to supplement her income. Now, she sees those financial burdens **as gifts in disguise: "It put me in a position to discover what I could do**," she says. With a fuller income, Marilyn could help her daughters live a more comfortable lifestyle.

Sarah's dream was always to become an interior designer. She entered a university in California and completed a degree in Interior Architectural Design. After college, Sarah was committed to creating an interior designing firm. She quickly realized the difficulties with traditional business. Little by little, the company grew. However, the work involved in the business was exhausting.

Meanwhile, Sarah watched as her mother achieved success in network marketing. She was shocked by the opportunities and the education involved in network marketing. She was drawn in. **"I saw the possibilities of where network marketing could take me,"** she says. "I always knew I would live an extraordinary lifestyle. I've always been able to dream big."

With network marketing, Sarah is able to fulfill her dreams. She has the financial freedom to choose her projects. Sarah is no longer controlled by her job. Now, she is entirely in control of her life.

Marilyn and Sarah Decided to Succeed

Marilyn was not a success immediately. "The president of our company says I was like a duck sitting on water. On the surface, I am an ordinary person. I live in a small city in southern Alberta, but my feet are moving a hundred miles an hour underneath me," she laughs. Even though she started slowly, Marilyn stayed focused on the learning curve. She recognized how much she needed to learn and set her mind to doing so.

Marilyn's **naivety** benefited her from the beginning. "I didn't know what I was stepping into. I just knew what I wanted to achieve. **I was an ordinary person willing to do what it takes,**" she reflects. She did not consider the possible downfall of failure and dived in headfirst.

Marilyn's **self-development** was essential to her success. She **enjoyed learning, and new possibilities opened up as she continued to grow**. Most importantly, she **decided** to seize these opportunities and take full advantage of her options.

With Marilyn as her mentor, Sarah learned as much as possible. She dealt with the learning curve as well, but she enjoyed the foundation that her mother had created. Sarah used her mother as a "spring board," but she knew that she had to create her own path. She recognized that nothing could be created over night. "I gave myself a couple of years," she remembers. "I knew time would tell." Slowly but surely, she became a shining example of success.

Marilyn and Sarah's Ingredients for Success

The dynamic duo willingly shares their success ingredients with others. Their strategies have worked for women across North America.

1. Be Optimistic

Have passion for the products and the company. Enthusiasm is contagious and spreads quickly.

2. Educate Yourself

Educate yourself about the products and the company. Attend meetings, read newsletters, and continue to grow. Learn about the compensation plans and the plans for success. A mentor is another great resource, even if she is not your mother!

If you are **open and willing to learn**, you will gain experience quickly. You can apply that experience and knowledge to your work. "**The amount you want to earn is a direct reflection of the effort you put in**," Marilyn says.

3. Stay Updated

Stay current in the company and the network marketing industry as a whole. You must be aware of the events that occur in your field.

4. Use Leverage

Use leverage to enroll more people. Duplicating your network can take time, so be patient.

5. Give Yourself Time

Many people assume that network marketing is more like a lottery than a field in which they can grow and develop. Marketing is a process, not something that can happen in a single day.

6. Help Others

Network marketing is first and foremost a **team**. **Your success is directly related to the success of others**. Develop your ability to work with others and to hone their skills. As Marilyn says, "**There is a constant rippling effect of everyone's success**."

7. Dream Big

In other jobs, there are specifications. You need to fit a certain mold. However, network marketing offers unlimited potential, regardless of age or education. Anyone can succeed. Marilyn and Sarah never put a limit to other people's successes. They instead helped people realize that, with a big WHY, anyone is capable of achieving their dreams.

Marilyn and Sarah's WHYs

Residual income is the WHY that enables Marilyn and Sarah to pursue their other interests. "Residual income is just an extraordinary concept when you look at it," Sarah says. "Once you get a taste of it, you realize it is really sweet." The perk of residual income is that as you raise the bar, your income increases as well. When she was a teacher, Marilyn thought an additional $2,000 per month was an impressive amount. Now, her financial opportunities are limitless.

One benefit of residual income for Marilyn and Sarah is that the two women can spend time helping others. Marilyn finds meaning in creating a platform for other people to succeed.

In doing so, she "influences and makes a difference in their physical and financial health."

Seeing success in other people's lives is a huge WHY for Marilyn. She is still a teacher at heart and she has given back by contributing to a leadership academy for children. Both women agree that funding and encouraging the "leaders of tomorrow" is the WHY that keeps them working hard every day.

The Mother and Daughter Team

Marilyn and Sarah enjoy a wonderful relationship. The two women have similar interests, and their personalities fit well together. The supportive relationship is clear by the way these two women are mentally and emotionally in sync.

For Marilyn, **having a positive relationship with her daughters was always very important**. **"I think we are on this planet learning life through relationships. So, you had better get it right with your family,"** she advises. Network marketing allows the family to work together, which both women agree has been a fun and positive experience.

Marilyn and Sarah's Legacies

Sarah's goal is to be a role model for others in her generation. She is passionate about showing people the opportunities that are available in network marketing. **"There are possibilities out there,"** she says confidently. **"There is a lot to look forward to rather than scarcity."** Her story has already helped numerous young people realize those possibilities in their own lives.

For Marilyn, the goal is to **mentor thousands of people by creating joy and kindness.** "**By touching one heart that touches another heart, we can make a difference on this planet,**" she says. As a top distributor in her company, Marilyn is already well on her way towards accomplishing that dream.

Kathy Aaron

Kathy's Background

For thirteen years, Kathy Aaron exhausted herself from sun up to sun down in the real estate business. Although she was quite successful, her holidays and vacations were never enjoyed; she was too concerned with the business while at home. Kathy felt guilty and believed that she should be working instead of enjoying her time off. "Everything revolved around the real estate business. I had no time freedom," Kathy said.

Then one day, on vacation in Montana, Kathy's life changed. Kathy found time to enjoy the beautiful scenery and to spend time outdoors. While gazing at the beautiful landscape, Kathy had an epiphany. Her youngest child had just left for college, and she finally realized there was so much more to life than work. Kathy realized that she had never owned a company; the company had always owned her. She left Montana ready to make a change.

Kathy Decided to Succeed

On her way home from Montana, Kathy spent many hours thinking. The trip to Montana provided enough beautiful scenery to absorb that she realized her 'enjoyment sponge' had been dry until now. She had always been so consumed with work that she had no time to enjoy the beauty of the world around her. During those hours of travel, she decided that she would find a way to get out from under the real estate business and begin living her life again.

Kathy knew that in order to run a successful business and work fewer hours, she would need a residual income. That was when Doug, a friend and former business associate, began campaigning for her to get into his home-based business.

Ironically, Kathy was reluctant to begin her journey into the network marketing industry that would ultimately earn her a fortune. Doug was a homebuilder who was struggling financially. He had been trying to convince Kathy to jump ship and come with him on this new venture.

Kathy empathized with Doug, saying, "The 80's were very hard for many people." She realized that he had already hit rock bottom and she did not want to go down the path he was on.

Kathy's WHY

Kathy's need to start living was her WHY. After her trip to Montana, her life changed. For the first time, during that vacation, she found a peace within herself that she had never known. Kathy knew that there was still so much more of the world that she had not seen. She wanted to seek out the beauty and majesty of other locations.

Kathy's reasons included:

- Buy her time back
- Earn a residual income
- Move to Montana
- Have an adventure

As a last resort, Kathy finally decided to give Doug's idea a shot, just in case network marketing was a way to fulfill her dream. Kathy's first informational event in the network marketing arena provided inspiration. Kathy saw thousands of motivated, excited business-minded professionals. She finally saw the bigger picture of the industry.

Kathy compared her first network marketing event with what she usually saw in her real estate events. There was no comparison. She immediately resigned from her real estate career and geared up for her first big adventure.

Kathy's Strengths

Kathy's success is a direct result of her ability to adapt to her surroundings. Kathy saw immediate success from day one, but she was not using the success model of network marketing: many people doing a little work.

Kathy blasted onto the scene by doing all of the work for her business. Kathy became a workaholic again and did most of the work on her own. When her immediate success did not duplicate easily, she realized she was still in real estate mode.

278

That is when she began modeling her home-based business after other successful businesses and top performers in the same arena – network marketing. She began to internalize the idea that, "If you build a team with many people doing their part to become successful, you can yield huge results." Kathy knew leadership skills were a necessity to succeed.

Kathy Decided to Succeed

Kathy Decided to Succeed. She knew she would have to make the necessary changes to move out of "real estate" mode, so she embarked on a daily self-development program.

Be Coachable and Teachable

Kathy turned her dwindling business around by becoming coachable and teachable. She started by putting aside her ego. She knew she had to forget that she was a top real estate sales person. She also had to forget all of her knowledge of marketing. Kathy pretended she did not know anything. She became a student of the industry and became a personal self-development freak. To do this, she:

- read every book she could find
- listened to audio books as much as possible
- attended many seminars

Model after Successful People

Kathy found a successful person in the industry and observed what this person did to become successful. Kathy worked with her mentor and modeled everything they were doing. Then she asked herself: what is this person doing to sustain success? Kathy found that mimicking the traits of successful network marketers allowed her to develop into a successful network marketer herself.

Adaptability

Kathy always strived to meet her expectations. If something was not working, Kathy attempted to find another way to tackle the problem. Kathy never stuck to a standard practice, especially a failing standard practice. A key ingredient to her success has been her willingness to learn from her mistakes and trust the system.

Kathy's Ingredients for Success

1. Select a Successful Team

Kathy surrounds herself with people who are either equally successful or more so than she was. Kathy surrounded herself with a group of leaders of the same or higher caliber to create her team. She also made every effort to clarify that the company was not *her* organization. Kathy referred to the company as 'OUR team.' By letting people know they are part of a team, Kathy created strong leaders within the group.

2. Encourage the Strengths of Others

Kathy strives to find what people are doing right, instead of zeroing in on what mistakes they have made. By encouraging other team members, she builds team morale and allowing others to see who they can go to if they need specific help. The team thrives off each person's strengths.

3. Listen to the WHY

Kathy discovers each team member's WHY. Knowing that a strong WHY created her own success, Kathy believes that all of her team members should also have a strong WHY. After all, the WHY is what keeps the team strong, as the WHY is the reason they joined and stayed in the business.

4. Flick Away Obstacles

When Kathy faces obstacles, she flicks them away like a fly. She strongly believes that nothing can stop her from accomplishing what she wants to accomplish. That mentality has saved her from breaking down on some of the rough days.

5. Find Team Members with a Strong Desire

Team members must have a desire. Desire is the starting point of all success in life. Kathy says, "If you are not launching some rocket of desire, not much is going to happen for you."

6. Learn from Mistakes

Kathy tells her team members about the mistakes she made early in her career. She also asks new team members if they are willing to let former team members or career retirees teach them. Kathy believes this commitment is important. From these experienced workers, they will learn to be teachable and coachable.

7. Create a Plan of Action
Kathy says, "The plan of action is your team's proven system. This is what you teach all of your team members." Kathy creates a weekly, monthly, and quarterly method of operation. That way, team members know what is expected of them. The more people locked into the system, the more of an advantage Kathy's team has. In turn, she believes her team will grow faster.

Kathy's Legacy

Kathy strives to become a better steward. She believes her WHY has changed and is now to develop business leaders. Kathy would like to inspire people and teach them that they can have whatever they want.

Kathy wants to develop as many leaders as possible, because leaders can:

- make changes in the market place
- make changes in their communities
- make changes in their families
- affect thousands of people
- become a better person

Kathy wants everyone to know that anything is possible; all that is needed is a little effort. Past failures should not determine future successes. No matter how many times a person has failed in the past, Kathy believes that their positive attitude and perseverance determine future success. She says, "borrow someone else's belief in you until you have that same belief in yourself."

Kathy hopes that through this teaching, she can reach enough people to cause a ripple effect. This ripple effect could affect generations to come.

Brenda Loffredo

Brenda's Background

Brenda Loffredo did not venture into network marketing at an early age. She grew up in a household that valued the traditional mindset of earning a degree, finding a job, and then making money and finding happiness. For many years, Brenda lived a decent lifestyle and committed to the traditional values that her parents instilled in her at a young age.

The decent lifestyle consisted of working many hours and traveling all of the time. Because she worked so hard, Brenda found that she became one of the first women to hold her positions in the corporate world. She also struggled with the glass ceiling that existed in the industry. Brenda always felt that she had to prove herself as a woman, which was one of the biggest stressors in her life.

Brenda Decided to Succeed

Everything turned around for Brenda when she had her son. She was 40 years old when she gave birth to her only child. At the beginning of her son's life, he was surrounded by nannies and nurses. Brenda's son spent a lot of time in and out of daycares. Brenda felt that she should be the one raising her son and began to question her lifestyle. She knew that she would only have one shot at raising her boy, and she wanted to raise him the right way.

Brenda wanted to devote more time and energy to her son than to her career. While she had this revelation, the corporate world started to change as well. She knew that she would not be able to do the job she had done before the birth of her son and still raise him in the way she saw fit. Brenda started looking for other options.

After leaving her corporate position, Brenda began her own consulting company. She quickly found that her 'corporate' hat had only been traded for a 'small business owner' hat. This new position was not giving her the freedom she wanted, so she began looking for other options. Brenda's small business was not the ideal place for her and she claims, "When you own a small business, the small business owns you."

She and her husband looked into some franchises, but hit a roadblock. Franchises are expensive, requiring hundreds of thousands to start. Franchises also presented a conflict with the age of those working around them; they did not want their livelihood entrusted to teenagers. The franchise was expensive to start and it would take up to five years to make a profit.

Then, Brenda began looking into the network marketing industry. Brenda found that she would not have to employ anyone and could arrange her own hours. She believed that this would alleviate stress.

To begin, Brenda and her husband tried their hands in a few companies. They worked part time with several companies before they found a good fit. Once they found a company they liked, they also found that they were given the freedom they were looking to find.

Brenda's venture was not successful immediately. She **Decided** she would succeed. She began to treat her network marketing business like a business. She decided to invest as much time and energy into network marketing as she would in any traditional business. She also made the decision that she was in it "for the long haul."

As her son got older, she found more flexibility with her time and decided to invest more time into her company. Brenda began investing a lot of time and money into her career, learning about the industry. With more experience under her belt, Brenda decided that she would rather sell a service than a product. She believed that she would make more money this way. This decision led her to the current company for which she works.

Several years passed before Brenda earned a six-figure income. Brenda and her husband wanted the process of starting a business to be more like a marathon than a sprint. She said that she wanted to build her business with a strong foundation, and to do this, she spent many years finding what would work best for her.

Brenda's WHY

Brenda and her husband wanted to be able to spend more time at home with their son. Brenda knew that she would only have one son and wanted to make sure she did everything correctly. She did not want her son to be raised by nannies and daycare workers.

Brenda's WHY also included getting away from corporate America. She worked for her company for nine years before taking the leap. Since then, Brenda has never looked back.

Brenda's Strengths

Brenda knew that her success depended on the effort that she put into the business. Brenda recognized the "unlimited potential" in network marketing, and she could tap into this potential by devoting her time to learning the industry.

Brenda was able to balance her home life with a new career. She was patient when waiting for success and never expected overnight success. This allowed her to continue pursuing her new career with little stress.

Brenda's Ingredients for Success

1. Identify the Person's WHY

The first thing Brenda does when she meets a new person is to help them identify what they want to accomplish, which gives the person motivation instantaneously. Brenda knows that anyone who is unclear of the vision or goals they have for themselves will quit after they hit the first obstacle. According to Brenda, taking the time to build the dream with new employees is worth every second.

2. Help Team Members Dream Again

Brenda believes that adults stop dreaming at some point. She strives to help people start dreaming again. Dreams have the tendency to propel children forward towards reaching their goals. She wants that childlike enthusiasm to resurface in her team members.

3. Uncover Fears

Identifying and hitting fears head on during the beginning stages of a new relationship allows the person to overcome those fears before being consumed by them. All people have fears. She wants to help eliminate them by shedding a little light in the dark place, wherever that place may be for that person.

4. Be Passionate about the Product

Brenda believes that talking about the products and services they provide creates more passion about the selling of those products. No one can be successful without a love of the product.

To ensure that all of her team members are passionate about the product, Brenda makes sure to be very clear about what they provide and how they help people.

5. Build Relationships

Brenda thinks of her customers and asks herself: how will the product benefit the customers? By empathizing with the needs of her customers, she has learned that she can effectively gain a large customer base.

Brenda's Legacy

Brenda would like to be known as a servant leader who helps others. Brenda finds more satisfaction by helping someone else reach his or her goals than she does focusing only on herself. Brenda recognizes that the more she can help others, the more help she will receive. She strives to make a difference with everyone she meets.

Barbara Freundt

Barbara's Background

Barbara Freundt spent the majority of her adult life working as a stay at home mother. With children of various ages, she was always busy. Barbara spent her days picking one child up from soccer practice and then rushing home to make sure the baby had dinner on time. One day, while using a product she knew and loved, Barbara's sister called her and asked if she had ever heard of a certain company. The company Barbara's sister referred to was the company that sold the product Barbara was using. Barbara's sister then described how she had recently become involved with the company as a home-based business.

As a savvy businesswoman, Barbara's sister pushed Barbara to get involved in the business as well. Barbara refused to allow her sister to continue talking to her about the business opportunity. She was not interested, because she knew that network marketing was involved. Barbara had negative assumptions about network marketing companies, although she never knew anyone in network marketing.

Barbara Decided to Succeed

Several months after the initial phone call from her sister, Barbara finally succumbed to her sister's requests to listen to the business opportunity. Barbara's sister set up a small, intimate meeting with just a few people. Everything Barbara saw and heard impressed her. The principles of network marketing rang true to her. The people were extremely impressive; Barbara liked their positive attitudes. She began questioning herself and asking, "If they can do this. Why can't I?"

Barbara looks back at this point in her decision-making process and believes that her naivety probably contributed to her involvement in the company. She jumped in with both feet.

In Barbara's mind, she was a success from day one. Barbara told herself, "I know I can make it. I know I will. There are no other options." Barbara knows that in network marketing and in life, half of the battle is overcoming a negative mindset. Her success stems from her mentality that, whatever she was going to do, she was going to succeed.

Barbara said, "I just **Decided** my goal in the beginning was to make $10,000 dollars a month. Once I made my decision, that was that, and it was easy for me. I woke up in the morning knowing what I had to do. I decided I had to meet 8 people a month, 2 per week. That's not a lot in this industry, but my family came first."

From then on, nothing held her back. She met with those people at lunchtime, so as not to interfere with her family time. "I am really bad with numbers, so my husband figured out that out of 8 people, 3 per month were joining me in my business. Those are pretty good odds," said Barbara. By the end of her first year, Barbara was seeing monetary results.

Barbara attributes her success to sheer determination. She truly had to train herself, as her sponsor was more than 700 miles away, and back then there were no computers. She just made appointments with new prospects, introduced them to the products and business, and enjoyed visiting with them. "I knew if I just kept meeting with people the numbers would begin to add up and it would all work out. I married someone who could handle the numbers, so I had the fun job of meeting with people," Barbara said.

Barbara's WHY

With Barbara's success starting early, she could focus more on her ability to provide for her family. Barbara started working in the network marketing industry because of her family. When she began, she had children getting ready to go off to college, and others were enrolled in private school. Barbara always wished that she could contribute more to the family, but knew that she was needed at home with the children. Network marketing was a great way for her to be able to work from home and contribute monetarily at the same time.

Now with all of her children out of school, Barbara focused her WHY elsewhere: her grandchildren. Barbara still helps her children as much as possible, but strives to make sure she does not overstep her boundaries. Barbara knows that "it's easy to take over their ambition to work" and tries to make them work for what they have.

Barbara's Strengths

Barbara's success stems from her determination and motivational self-talk. She never allowed herself to think of failure and repeatedly focused on a goal and pushed forward until she succeeded. Then, a new goal would be set, and she pushed forward until that goal was reached.

Breaking her success into mini goals, Barbara found that work never seemed stressful. Because of this, she has never been overwhelmed by the enormity of her success.

Barbara's Ingredients for Success

1. Never Pre-Judge
Barbara looks for the 'go-getters.' People who strive to reach their goals regardless of the obstacles they face are perfect fits for her company. Barbara says she has found many of these people in unexpected places: "I'll meet someone I never expected to work, but they will work. On the flipside, I'll meet someone and think they will work, but who failed." She learned never pre-qualify someone, because doing so will always prove to be incorrect.

2. Education
Barbara frequently reads books and checks the Internet for new information about her business. By continuing her

education, she stays one step ahead of those who only rely on traditional knowledge.

And then... Barbara was diagnosed with cancer. This could have been devastating for anyone else but Barb knew just what to do. She swung into action. Her home-based business allowed her the freedom to stay at home and take care of herself. Unlike a traditional corporation job, Barb could choose when to work and when to rest. The stress of going out to a job did not exist so she was free to spend her time finding the exact way for her to heal.

Barb's basic knowledge of medicine, learned in the course of her home-based business, helped her decide the route she would take for her treatment. With an interest in natural healing practices, she began to research treatment options extensively.

Barbara visited twelve doctors; six practiced Western medicine, and six practiced natural healing methods. She listened, she learned and she finally knew enough to maintain an integral role in her own cancer treatment.

While currently battling the cancer, Barbara remains extremely optimistic that her determination, her optimistic outlook and her continuing self-education will help her win the fight.

Barbara's Legacy

Barbara wants to be remembered as an integral member of the network marketing industry who never cut corners. She used her integrity and work ethic to earn her success. When Barbara looks back at her career and remembers that she pushed to the top in an honest way, she feels the pride of a truly accomplished woman.

Barbara's true legacy is her family. Her optimistic outlook, loving spirit, and determined nature shine through her children and grandchildren.

Marcella Vonn Harting

Marcella's Background

Marcella is an amazing woman and one of the top earners in her company. She is an internationally renowned author, speaker, and facilitator. Marcella has taught women in the United States, Canada, Australia, Japan, and all over Europe. She lives with her husband and two children in Paradise Valley, Arizona.

Before her success in network marketing, Marcella was a housewife and mother. One day, she experienced a traumatic event that drastically changed the course of her life forever. At birth, her daughter swallowed Meconium, a tar-like substance that is a baby's first bowel movement, which penetrated her lungs. Physicians suctioned her lungs for six and a half hours. For 12 days, Marcella and her husband lived in the children's critical care department at St. Joseph's Hospital. At seven months of age, Marcella's daughter clinically died in her husband's arms, as they rushed to the hospital. Physicians miraculously managed to revive her, but the event changed Marcella's outlook on life forever.

The doctors advised Marcella that her daughter would need to be institutionalized and would probably suffer horrible brain damage. Marcella kicked into action and went on a search. She focused her attention on the health and nutrition field, hoping to find a holistic solution for her daughter. Her search led her to the network marketing industry, where she discovered amazing companies with even more amazing products. These companies invested their money on superior ingredients that produced highly researched products, which were far superior to the often additive and synthetic chemical laden store-bought products.

Marcella Decided to Succeed

Marcella's focus was **on the network marketing products she had discovered and how they could help her little girl.** She had no desire to build a business. Being a mom was her top priority. Her husband made a good living in their Burger King franchise. His family had been involved in the business for 40 years, so Marcella used their family as a role model.

Marcella began telling everyone who would listen about the miraculous products that were helping her beloved daughter and family. People started ordering her products. She never expected to earn a steady income; she just wanted to help others avoid illness. When she and her husband received a W-9 form that year, they were astonished. She had earned over $200,000!

Marcella already lived a comfortable lifestyle and was shocked by how much money she was beginning to make. She realized the potential of her business, and her attitude changed. More importantly, she compared her network marketing business with her husband's traditional business. Without employees or insurance, her business did not face the same obstacles. The more she learned, the more she embraced network marketing.

When Marcella made the decision to build and support her organization, she created a newsletter to stay in touch with people and to inform them of the benefits of the products. She made herself totally accessible to her organization and offered a money back guarantee. Once her educational newsletter came out, Marcella's business flourished. This approach is much different from that of other distributors. "I was not coming at it from the angle of selling or money-making," she says.

Although Marcella achieved success by following a unique route, she had her fair share of challenges. She struggled with a stuttering challenge for years, which made speaking to others difficult. Instead of feeling defeated, Marcella felt motivated to conquer her stuttering challenge. "**Whatever you struggle with the most is what you came to this planet to do,**" she asserts. Her desire to conquer her speech challenge motivated her to succeed instead of holding her back.

Marcella's greatest passion, however, was learning how to reach people. She wanted to learn their desires. She wanted to show them how to achieve their dreams and goals. According to Marcella, "**There are two reasons why people do things: either to gain pleasure or to avoid pain.**" In an effort to avoid pain, many people tend to sabotage themselves. Marcella chose to guide people towards gaining pleasure.

Marcella's Strengths

Marcella knew how to share her product throughout her warm market and to establish new relationships in the process. Her first step was to share the products with other mothers. The school teachers at her daughter's school were baffled – how could Marcella raise her daughter without going to a traditional job every day? So, Marcella shared the products with her friends at the school. She readily accepted offers to be introduced to new people. In this way, Marcella never had to advertise or use a cold market. She depended on word-of-mouth to build up her warm market.

Marcella's greatest strength, however, is her ability to follow up. She wrote **thank-you notes by hand** and always thanked people for their time, no matter the outcome. In the "**go-where-you-know business**" of network marketing, these follow-up notes made all the difference. Marcella **wrote from the heart** and established personal relationships.

Marcella's Ingredients for Success

Marcella uses a five-step system that helps her business grow.

1. Focus on the Relationships
As an event leader, Marcella was chosen to work with Tony Robbins. As a result, she received phenomenal training and

applied her new skills to her work. "I literally took what I learned and started to apply it to the psychology of working with people in my organization and business," she says. By putting effort into building relationships, Marcella's business boomed.

2. Build Rapport

Marcella teaches people how to build rapport with others by being supportive. A person's choice whether to use the products or to be involved in the company should not affect your friendship with them. If the timing isn't right, stay in touch anyway. For Marcella, teaching is more important than selling. As a mentor, she advises **people to think about the big picture.** She even invites people from all over the world to mentor with her for several days. They have the chance to see her lifestyle and the everyday work involved in network marketing.

3. Focus on the WHY

Marcella never focused on HOW. Instead her WHY motivated her to keep working, no matter the challenge.

4. Create Leverage

Marcella's most important advice is to **never quit.** Many people give up after a bad day. **"If we can keep them in action, most will see success,"** she says. According to Marcella, **there is a magic number that can motivate people to stay in the business: 300. If someone earns $300 in 90 days, they are much more likely to stay with you, even if challenges arise.**

5. Live What You Talk

Marcella invites people to mentor with her over a several day period. During that time, she provides resources and gives an overview of the industry. She instructs people on how to listen and how to build rapport skills. Each morning, Marcella starts the lessons with a walk to help people take care of their bodies first. In doing so, Marcella practices what she preaches: "For me personally, I can do more than just talking with people. It's the way I live my life. I walk my talk?"

Marcella's WHY

Marcella's daughter inspired her to become involved in network marketing. Now, at age 25, her daughter is the youngest distributor at the "gold" level in her company. Marcella's son is 21 years old and is the youngest distributor at the "silver" level. Together, their family can support one another. They never have to punch a clock. "Our children have picked up on the lifestyle," she says. "I am doing what I'm doing for the legacy of my children. They are very much involved." Marcella's WHY is her love for her children.

Marcella's Legacy

Motherhood comes first for Marcella. Her life is dedicated towards providing a nurturing and loving environment for her children. Marcella hopes to leave the planet as a place where her children feel grounded and safe. "My greatest gift is being a mother," she says. Her life is centered on her kids, and they are her legacy.

Holly Warnol

Holly's Background

Holly Warnol never imagined she would be in the network marketing industry. As a stay-at-home mom, her focus was on her two children. Holly also wanted to be an attractive wife, but she always struggled with acne-prone skin. Using products made her skin break out even more. She became desperate. When an old high school friend suggested she try a new product, Holly skeptically took a chance. She was ecstatic when the product worked.

For six months, Holly was an enthusiastic product user. "When I learned that it was not only what you eat but also what you put on your skin that affects your health, I was astonished. It makes a difference and has long-term effects. My enthusiasm turned to passion to get the word out," said Holly.

She did not know about the business side of the company and decided to attend an event. The education she gained within those few hours changed Holly's life. **"I came out with clear intention,"** Holly remembers. **"I put a plan of action together. I had the intent to build a business, rather than living like it was a hobby."** The business side clicked. Holly saw other women prospering, and she was confident that she could do the same.

Holly Decided to Succeed

The friend who had sponsored Holly did not live near her. Even without close support from her, Holly **Decided** to "make it work." She needed to generate an extra $500 a month to cover car payments. With this goal in mind, Holly immediately started working. Her results did not show up until a couple of months later. "People don't understand that delayed results are normal in this industry. Be patient," says Holly. When her checks started to double, she knew that the business was the real deal.

With her faith in God and her church as support, Holly had never cared much about self-development. However, she suddenly recognized that she had to build belief in the company and in herself. Her ideas changed. She wanted to learn everything she could about personal growth and network marketing. Then, her husband Rich had his light bulb moment. The couple realized that their new business would **"be the million dollar gift everyone talks about."** Holly was more determined than ever to share her story and to help others.

Holly's Ingredients for Success

Holly's five-step plan helps to simplify an industry that can sometimes be very complex.

1. Know What You Want

Each person has different individual goals. Some want to make extra cash in addition to their incomes. Others want to replace their incomes as soon as possible. People's goals will determine how many hours need to be put in, and your role is to **help people achieve their goals.**

2. Develop a Plan

Holly advises each person to **write out specific goals** and a plan for achieving those goals. Even in the early stages, a person will feel motivated when they **"start to see little successes and little victories."**

3. Set Goals

Set goals that can be easily achieved. When the person reaches those goals, reward them with praise. The more a person can feel accomplished and appreciated, the more motivated they will feel.

4. Use the Products

The only way to learn about the products is to use them as frequently as possible. Instead of going to a store to purchase your personal care products, purchase products from your own company. You can earn while you learn by using the products. Once your home is converted into your personal store, you can speak with more authority on the subject.

5. Start the Activity

Pick up the phone. Schedule appointments. Speak with as many people as possible to make your business really boom.

Holly's Strengths

Three main attributes help Holly in her business endeavor. First, she has a passion for the products and for the company. She loves her job and enjoys working every day. Her team has happy hours, lunches, and picnics. Second, she is confident. People are attracted to confidence. They are eager to learn more about the company if they feel they can boost their own confidence in doing so. Lastly and most importantly, Holly enjoys helping others. By putting others first, Holly continues to build a network of encouraging, supportive people.

Holly's WHY

Financial need was originally Holly's WHY. As her business thrived, her WHY started to incorporate other people's WHYs as well. Her family and friends became involved in her business. Holly regularly says to people, **"Your WHY has to be big enough to keep you up at night and get you up in the morning."** Holly's WHY is now very focused on other people's WHYs.

Holly's Legacy

Holly's motto is "Make a Difference," based on the popular film *Cool Runnings*. Her legacy will always be making a difference with determination, belief, and action all while having fun. Holly wakes up every morning with the hope of impacting as many lives as possible. This strong and persistent woman is well on her way towards fulfilling that goal.

Susan Walsh

Susan's Background

As the owner of a hair salon for over 27 years, Susan Walsh has always been an entrepreneur. For the past two decades, Susan has been a force to reckon with in the network marketing industry. She and Gary, her husband of 38 years, have lived a dream life with their children and grandchildren. Although her story is a happy one, Susan had to overcome many challenges to be the successful businesswoman she is today. Success isn't convenient!

Susan always had a great work ethic, which was instilled in her by her father. After 10 years, her hard work paid off when she reached a six-figure income at her hair salon. Unfortunately, she created her own personal prison in the process. Susan felt trapped in her gilded cage and had no exit plan. She worked over 80 hours a week. She raised two amazing sons and "watched them grow up through a video camera." Susan's life was spinning out of control and she desperately needed a change, but how do you walk away from a six-figure income?

The change happened when Susan's son proudly announced his acceptance into medical school. Susan was genuinely thrilled, but her heart sank at the same time. She was not prepared to shell out an additional $5,000 a month. After that moment, Susan was open to almost any possibility that came along so that her son could live his dream of becoming a doctor.

Oddly enough, no one had ever presented a network marketing opportunity to Susan. She knew nothing about the concept. One day, a customer introduced Susan to the product side of network marketing. He told her she could buy products at wholesale prices and sell them in her salon for retail. She was interested from the start. "I could literally sell in my salon and bring in a bit more income without lots more effort," she says. She was hooked. To complete the company's paperwork, she had to drive more than 100 miles, but that did not stop her. Susan dove in and earned an extra $5,000 a month within a short time.

Susan Decided to Succeed

One day, Susan received an unexpected call from an anonymous man. He asked how long she had been involved in network marketing and how she was progressing. "I'm buying wholesale and selling retail. I guess everything is going okay," she responded.

Several days later, the man visited her and shared his story. He opened the door to endless possibilities by teaching Susan about the business side of network marketing and how she could receive a percentage of what other people earned as well. Susan inquisitively asked, "You mean I can get a percentage of what other people earn, too? How is that possible?" He replied, "If you will be coachable and teachable and follow my lead, I'll take you where you want to go."

In all her years with the salon no one had ever offered to help her do anything, much less make a significant income and change her life at the same time. Without batting an eye, Susan took a chance and accepted him as a mentor. She told him, "I know nothing about this industry! What I bring is a tremendous work ethic and a PhD in People. If you can do something with that, I will be teachable. Mold me!"

Susan's mentor immediately put her on a **personal growth path**. When Susan complained that she didn't have time to read or to work on herself, he taught her how to reshape her life. **"Your income growth will never exceed your personal growth,"** he informed her. Susan went on a mission to improve and became **"hungry for knowledge."** Every day was a new journey for her – to live is to improve.

The doors to success did not fling open immediately. Susan made multiple mistakes and called her mentor daily for help. She did what most newcomers do, and begged people to join her business. "I had been like a water hose, hosing them down and drowning them with my products and company. My mentor helped me see that it's not about what I want, it's about what they want. **People buy benefits, not products**," Susan says. Her willingness to request help enabled her to learn and grow. She kept a positive attitude and reaffirmed her commitment over and over again.

Susan's Ingredients for Success

Susan's breaks down her **business philosophy** into the following eight steps:

1. Discover the WHY

To figure out whether or not you are capable of helping someone, learn WHY they want to join the business. **A person's WHY is the key to success or failure. You must have many reasons "Why" so that the "how to's" don't matter.**

2. Be Prepared to Hear No

Susan understands that "no's" come fast and in all shapes and sizes, and that most of the time it's not a "no," it is an "I don't "know" enough to make a decision. **The best way to handle a "no" is to bring the person's attention back to their WHY. Their HOW does not matter.**

3. Build a Business Plan

To build a successful business plan, cater each plan to the individual's needs. Consider the number of hours they are willing to work, their commitment level, and the financial investment they are willing to make. Overall, **the business plan should match the person's WHY. "If you treat this like a business, it will pay you like a business," Susan says. "If you treat this like a hobby, it is going to cost you money."**

4. Build Belief

Many people enter network marketing with a traditional business mindset. They expect to be told what to do in order to earn a salary. Furthermore, people expect immediate results. "I believe that if you help someone build their three-day story within their first 72 hours, you will help them build belief much quicker," Susan advises. Praise them to profits, and catch them doing it right! Babies cry for it, men die for it ... it's called love and recognition.

5. Move to Action

"Where there is no action, there is no friction. Where there is no friction, there are no results," Susan says. Show people how to jumpstart their business by getting them into immediate action, and the results will follow.

6. The Board of Directors

When a new person joins her business, Susan asks them to decide whom they would like on their "Board of Directors," people they have respect for, not influence over. Those "difference makers" in the community can inspire people to think differently and be open to the possibilities of owning their own business. Whether those respected people are doctors or teachers, each new person needs to model themselves after someone of influence that walks their talk. Success leaves clues!

7. Follow a Path of Exposure

Immediately place yourself in the midst of business owners, chamber events, and a variety of meetings. Start enrolling people as soon as possible, because momentum is critical in network marketing. A great goal is to sponsor 12 people in the first month, not one person per month in the first 12 months.

8. Plug into a System
Each new consultant should follow the company's system. The step-by-step path repeatedly shows new people how to develop and grow. Duplication is the key to a long-term, thriving residual income in network marketing.

Susan's WHY

Susan has added to her "WHY" over the years and has **had her vision stretched** in doing so. "**If your why is not constantly growing, how can you lead others? If your vision is not bigger than mine, you cannot lead me,**" she maintains. Susan is constantly realizing the limitless possibilities in network marketing and that anyone can do well in this business if they choose to be consistent and persistent.

Susan's Legacy
Susan wants to be recognized as a loving **wife and mother**. Her most important goal is to keep her husband happy and smiling. Plus, she strives to inspire her children and grandchildren and **lead by example**. In doing so, she has established a supportive environment and has taught her children to make excellent decisions and that there are absolutely no boundaries they can't cross.

Susan's legacy will also be as a **business woman who makes a difference in the world**. As a woman who spreads hope to others, she knows how to pay it forward: **"I am a pioneer in this new journey."** People all over the world have learned to enjoy life and to recognize their own self worth because of Susan's influence. She constantly strives to become the person others will follow!

Author's Note

It has been my true delight to work with the extraordinary women of the Women's Millionaire club. I am grateful to each and every one of them for sharing their Gift of Possibilities so graciously. It is my hope that their stories have educated, empowered and energized you. All who wish to increase productivity and unleash the millionaire inside need only **decide** to do so. These women also generously shared their Secret Recipes – now it's your turn to cook up a Batch of Success. Make the Impossible, Possible. Claim Your Destiny. Join the Club!

Join the Club: www.TheWomensMillionaireClub.com

Appendix
Terry Anna ~ PDP®

Terry Anna is a certified Professional DynaMetric Programs (PDP®) Consultant.

Terry helps organizations and home based businesses tap into the human potential inherent in their organization for greater productivity, job satisfaction and ultimately higher profit. He and his wife, Carolyn, provide expertise in personality 'success' assessments, job modeling, effective hiring and team productivity using PDP® applications.

MGM & Terry have developed a Success System:
- A statistically accurate one-of-a-kind 'Top Performer' profile to determine whether a prospect has the matching behavioral traits, energy levels and energy styles to become a top performing home-based business entrepreneur
- A 'Self-Development' Plan of Action
- Success Sessions ~'How To' Attract and Sponsor Top Performers
- Top Performer Coaching

For Information Regarding The Women's Millionaire Club Assessment & Success System contact the Exclusive Women's Millionaire Club PDP® Representative Terry Anna. **Mention 'The Women's Millionaire Club' for your Club Discount.**

PDP® Exclusive Women's Millionaire Club Representative
Contact: Terry Anna, CDMP Telephone: 970-222-9650
email: tanna@lpbroadband.net Website: www.mgmsuperstar.com

314

About the Author

Maureen Gail Mulvaney certainly lives up to her initials: MGM ... a Big Production.

MGM is a multi-faceted professional speaker and author who has spoken from Finland to Malaysia and in every corner of the USA. Her audiences encompass a broad spectrum of participants from all walks of life.

MGM is the author of *The Women's Millionaire Club: Success Recipes of Millionaire Women Entrepreneurs, The Stress Strategist, Any Kid Can Be a Super Star, Stinky David* and co-author of *Chicken Soup for the Teacher's Soul, and Mission Possible.*

MGM is a super star in her own right, as she has earned the highly coveted National Speaker's Association CSP – Certified Speaking Profession designation. Only the top 10% of all speakers around the world have earned CSP designation. One must have both longevity in the speaking industry and outstanding skills--MGM has both! She has also been a private practice therapist, psychology college instructor, public relations executive, and special and elementary educator.

MGM's action-packed presentations receive rave reviews. Every presentation is a blend of rich content and personal anecdotes to provide an entertaining, yet valuable learning experience. You'll laugh and learn!

To order products designed for the home-based business entrepreneur visit: www.TheWomensMillionaireClub.com, a website to educate, empower, and energize all home-based business women, small business, direct sales, network marketing, MLM marketing, and entrepreneurs.

> "Og Mandino, Zig Ziglar, Mark Victor Hansen, Danielle Kennedy, Patricia Fripp, and Mary Lou Henner... have all graced the Arbonne Stage. Clearly one name that stands out in the "who's who" list of International speakers is Maureen G. Mulvaney, MGM! **MGM** has been one of Arbonne's **highest rated HIRED speakers ever!**"
>
> I highly recommend MGM as the #1 speaker to motivate and move your people to the next level."
>
> Rita Davenport
> President –
> Arbonne International

Contact MGM to speak for your next event:
Call (800) 485-0065 or (480) 759-6251.
Email: mgm@mgmsuperstar.com
Speaker & Assessment Website: www.mgmsuperstar.com
www.TheWomensMillionaireClub.com

Earnings Disclaimer

Every effort has been made to represent the direct selling home-based business industry and its potential accurately. Even though this industry is one of the few where one can write their own check in terms of earnings, there is NO GUARANTEE that you will earn any money using the techniques and ideas in these materials. Examples in these materials are not to be interpreted as a promise or guarantee of earnings. Earning potential is entirely dependent on the person using these ideas, techniques and recipes for success. We do not purport this as a "get rich scheme."Any claims made of actual earnings or examples of actual results can be verified upon request.

Materials in our product and our website may contain information that includes or is based upon forward-looking statements within the meaning of the securities litigation reform act of 1995. Forward-looking statements give our expectations or forecasts of future events. You can identify these statements by the fact that they do not relate strictly to historical or current facts. They use words such as "anticipate," "estimate," "expect," "project," "intend," "plan," "believe," and other words and terms of similar meaning in connection with a description of potential earnings or financial performance.

Any and all forward looking statements here or on any of our sales material are intended to express our opinion of earnings potential. Many factors will be important in determining your actual results and no guarantees are made that you will achieve results similar to ours or anybody else's, in fact no guarantees are made that you will achieve any results from our ideas and techniques in our material.

Your level of success in attaining the results claimed in our materials depends on the time you devote to your business, ideas and techniques mentioned, your finances, knowledge and various skills. Since these factors differ according to individuals, we cannot guarantee your success or income level. Nor are we responsible for any of your actions.

The Secret Recipe For SUCCESS!

·KNOW WHAT YOU WANT.
Explore and clarify your thoughts.

·BELIEVE YOU CAN HAVE IT.
Examine and understand your beliefs and feelings.

·TAKE ACTION.
Learn to act appropriately and consistently.

·GIVE THANKS.
Appreciate your results.

Notes:

Notes: